W9-DBE-471

DISCARDED

*The Social Situation of Women
in the Novels of Ellen Glasgow*

THE
SOCIAL SITUATION
OF WOMEN
IN THE NOVELS OF
ELLEN GLASGOW

Elizabeth Gallup Myer

An Exposition-University Book
EXPOSITION PRESS
HICKSVILLE, NEW YORK

UPSALA COLLEGE LIBRARY
WIRTHS CAMPUS

PS
3513
L34
Z73

Excerpts from the works of Ellen Glasgow are reprinted with the kind permission of Harcourt Brace Jovanovich, Inc.

First Edition

© 1978 by Elizabeth Gallup Myer

All rights reserved, including the right of reproduction in whole or in part, in any form or by any means, electronic or mechanical, including photocopying, recording, or by any information storage and retrieval system. No part of this book may be reproduced without permission in writing from the publisher. Inquiries should be addressed to Exposition Press, Inc., 900 South Oyster Bay Road, Hicksville, N.Y. 11801

Library of Congress Catalog Card Number: 78-59460

ISBN 0-682-49165-9

Printed in the United States of America

To my parents

3984

Contents

I. OVERVIEW   11

II. HER LIFE   20

III. THE LITERARY AND SOCIAL BACKGROUNDS OF THE NOVELS   24

IV. A REALIST LOOKS AT THE SOUTH   33

V. CATEGORIES   36
Social Situation   36
Economical Situation   55
Political Situation   62
Religious Situation   63
Educational Situation   67

VI. CONCLUSION   72

SELECTED BIBLIOGRAPHY   74
Works of Ellen Glasgow   74
Bibliographies   75
Biographies   76
Commentaries   76
History   79
Chronological List of Novels   79

SUPPLEMENTAL BIBLIOGRAPHY   80
Works of Ellen Glasgow   80
Bibliography   80
Commentaries   80

The Social Situation of Women
in the Novels of Ellen Glasgow

I
Overview

The entry of woman into the highways and byways of modern endeavor—science, art, literature, politics, business, and education, even the Armed Forces—is still fresh enough in its novelty to stimulate wonder and curiosity on the means by which she arrived there, comparatively speedily, after generations of restraint. Her current freedom might be attributed directly and wholly to the effects of war, or wars, of which our country has had an abundance. Such deduction would slight the efficacy of the written word to bring about more generous attitudes toward the social situation of women.

One of the iconoclasts who skeptically appraised the social situation of women and satirically assailed it in her novels, in order to help make their freedom, was Ellen Glasgow. According to all rules of logic, Ellen Glasgow should have been content to live quietly in Richmond society, as a cultivated, Southern aristocrat, and to ignore the problems of her day. Fortunately she was avid for information; she absorbed facts and legends of the past, grew up observant of times and conditions, sought an intelligent meaning for life, and, from early youth, felt constrained to express her beliefs and protests. Instead of retreating into the sheltered security of a comfortable home, Miss Glasgow bent a critical eye upon postbellum Virginia, and stated her opinions in print at intervals over forty-six years; she asserted in caustic or subtle or witty or sympathetic terms the plight of woman not only in Virginia but in the world.

Through the medium of fiction Ellen Glasgow built up a case for the emancipation of woman from bondage to the Victorian ideal. Her gallery of ladies who depend upon the gallant attentions of gentlemen and of middle-class women who can fend for themselves furnishes a true history of the emancipation of women in the United States.

Miss Glasgow's accomplishments could mark other notable milestones in the progress of the American novel: its penetration in characterization, its growth in technique, and its grasp, at last, on reality. This appraisal, however, focuses upon her inclusive presentation of the social situation of women—in the South, to be sure, but typical of other supposedly civilized parts of the country or of the world, where society has failed to see woman as an individual.

In adopting a setting of Kingsborough (Williamsburg), or of Queensborough (Richmond), or of Dinwiddie (Petersburg), the author did not limit her vision to the South, but delivered a universal interpretation of life through a locale which she knew most intimately:

> Human nature in this town of twenty-one thousand inhabitants differed from human nature in London or in the Desert of Sahara mainly in the things that it ate and the manner in which it carried its clothes. The same passions stirred its heart, the same instincts moved its body, the same contentment with things as they are, and the same terror of things as they might be, warped its mind.[1]

In following Miss Glasgow's narratives, it requires only a little imagination for us to note the now obsolete obstacles to full living, to realize the dogmatic canons of conduct inflexibly laid down by the stronger sex and docilely adhered to by the weaker. The domination of women by men, with its attendant negations, abuses, and tragedies illustrated the Victorian ideal of subjection which led women to frustration. We expect to find in the nineteen novels of Ellen Glasgow emphasis upon the social advance of women, from shackled, mental inertness to intellectual, economic, political, and social freedom. The subjection of women to men's ideas has long since given way to the independence allowed women in our time, because of pressure from war and because of enlightened opinion for which Miss Glasgow's work was partly responsible.

Ellen Glasgow did not draw all her heroines from the privileged class, although she did have a special knack for penetrating the admirable exterior of a Southern belle like Virginia Pendleton, in *Virginia*, and for analyzing the unselfishness and sense of duty which sustain such a radiant creature throughout a sterile life. On the other hand, some of her most memorable characters come from the middle class of stern Scotch-Irish ancestry, what Miss Glasgow calls the "good people"—heroines like Dorinda Oakley in *Barren Ground* (1925) and Ada Fincastle in *Vein of Iron* (1935), who will not allow themselves to be subdued by circumstance. They survive desertion by their lovers, the stigma of "fallen women," and still persevere in their determination to get satisfaction from life, if not in the rewards of happiness, at least in the pride of endeavor. Dorinda masters farming, and attains prosperity. Gabriella, in *Life and Gabriella* (1916), liberates herself from a weakling husband, and succeeds as a milliner. The heroines encountered in these novels are not always conformists like Virginia Pendleton. Frequently they are rebels, refusing to do what is expected of them. They often dare to assert their own opinions, to engage in new fields of activity, to disregard social restraints, and to act as independent individuals in a free society.

These once radical ideas of feminine freedom affronted provincial society. The first novel, *The Descendant*, published anonymously in 1897, was attributed to a man. In 1900 *The Voice of the People*, Miss Glasgow's first strong book, rent the anonymity and the illusions of Richmond friends. In these novels Ellen, a young unmarried woman, had broken with American precedent by writing of unpleasant matters, about an illegitimate hero and socialism. From the publication of *The Voice of the People* forward, the Virginia author could expect disapproval from conservative Southerners, but serious consideration from the critics and a discerning public.

Steadily, additional novels reached a widening circle of readers. For a while, after the publication of *The Battle-Ground*, in 1902, the public associated her with the historical romancers, despite the wide gulf between her treatment of the Civil War

and the methods of Mary Johnston, John Esten Cooke, or Thomas
Nelson Page. *The Deliverance* in 1904, *The Ancient Law* in
1908, *The Romance of a Plain Man* in 1909, and *The Miller of
Old Church* in 1911 placed her temporarily in the ranks of the
local colorists, or regional writers. Again classification of this
mystifying Southerner shifted with the arrival of *Virginia*, in
1913, which had all the attributes of a perfect comedy of manners.

Frederic Taber Cooper boldly affirmed, in 1911, that she
outranked Gertrude Atherton or Edith Wharton.[2] Six years later,
Joyce Kilmer admired her "optimism that is genuine and robust."[3]
A fellow Virginian, James Branch Cabell, evinced faith in her
from the beginning of her career, and identified her as "a poet
in grain,"[4] and as "the foremost woman novelist of America."[5]
Barren Ground, in 1925, assured Miss Glasgow's preeminence
once and for all. H. L. Mencken spoke of her "acute . . . and
civilized mind."[6] Dorothea Lawrance Mann considered *Barren
Ground* the "epic novel."[7] Henry Seidel Canby nominated her
"as our best contemporary master of the tragic drama of significant manners."[8] Douglas Southall Freeman, long prejudiced in
her favor, said her realism "is that of unflinching fidelity to those
aspects of life her interest, her taste, and her uprearing lead her
to describe."[9] Nellie Elizabeth Monroe would seem to be dis-
missing her too lightly as "an excellent minor novelist . . . the
passion and urgency of life are left out, except in *Barren Ground*,
and her sympathy is not deep enough to celebrate the passing
of an era."[10] "She does not drop deep enough into her characters
to move the heart."[11] Miss Monroe, we can say, is in the minority,
and, furthermore, fails to substantiate her critical arguments.
Stuart Sherman and other critics have devoted much space in
recent years to serious, appreciative appraisal of this novelist
who has held her own so gracefully with the passing of time.

Instead of retiring crowned with glory for *Barren Ground*,
Ellen Glasgow did an about face from the somber locale and
theme to resume her comedy of manners in *The Romantic
Comedians*, 1926, and *They Stooped to Folly*, 1929. Nearing
sixty in 1932, she brought out with unflagging vitality her tragi-
comedy, *The Sheltered Life*. When the impressive *Vein of Iron*

appeared in 1935, it seemed unthinkable that the Pulitzer Prize Committee should again pass her by. Nevertheless, it did. Not until the publication of *In This Our Life*, in 1941, did the committee vote favorably and grant at last a long-deserved honor. Fortunately other recognition was less tardy. In 1930 the University of North Carolina bestowed an honorary Doctor of Letters upon her; in 1938 the University of Richmond and Duke University acclaimed her with an honorary Doctor of Laws; a year later the College of William and Mary honored her similarly, and gave her honorary membership in the Phi Beta Kappa Society. In 1940 the American Academy of Arts and Letters significantly awarded her the Quinquennial Howells Medal for "eminence in creative literature as shown in the novel." Also in this year *The Saturday Review of Literature* honored her with a special award for distinguished service to American Literature. In 1941 she received the Southern Authors Prize. It is evident that Miss Glasgow came to be well appreciated during her lifetime.

By 1929 Doubleday, Doran and Company thought it timely to begin a definitive edition of her best novels and by 1933 had completed the Old Dominion Edition in eight volumes: *The Voice of the People, The Battle-Ground, The Deliverance, The Miller of Old Church, Virginia, Barren Ground, The Romantic Comedians,* and *They Stooped to Folly.* A more distinguished and complete edition, limited by subscription ($140), appeared in 1938 under the imprint of Scribner, and numbered twelve volumes: *Barren Ground, The Miller of Old Church, Vein of Iron, The Sheltered Life, The Romantic Comedians, They Stooped to Folly, The Battle-Ground, The Deliverance, Virginia, The Voice of the People, The Roman of a Plain Man,* and *Life and Gabriella.* Two salutary facts may be noticed in connection with these sets: Miss Glasgow did whatever revising and cutting seemed advisable, thus preserving the full strength and form of the original, and the issuance of definitive editions during her lifetime, rather than posthumously, offers genuine proof of the high esteem with which this author was regarded.

Few novelists extend their productivity over forty-six years.

Fewer still have been capable of approaching this record without relaxing or diminishing the quality of the output. Although not very strong in health, yet adhering to strict rules of revision that cost time and energy, Ellen Glasgow turned out nineteen novels—of which twelve or thirteen have especial merit—a book of prefaces to these novels, a book of short stories, and one of verse.

A life passed between the years 1874 and 1945 included diverse currents, trends, and reactions. Added to her living observations, Ellen Glasgow acquired an inheritance of antebellum impressions, stories, and legends which she used to advantage in her earliest novels, *The Voice of the People*, *The Battle-Ground*, and *The Deliverance*. The period comes to life so completely and perfectly that the reader feels as if he were getting a contemporaneous account. The author may therefore be said to have projected a social history of her native state, antedating her own years. *The Battle-Ground* begins in 1850, amid the luxury, gracious living, and complacency of plantation life. It follows through the gathering of war clouds, secession, bitter realities of war, into the fiasco of defeat. *The Deliverance* covers the Reconstruction era; specifically, 1878 to 1890. *The Voice of the People* traces its hero's rise from the common people during the period 1870 to 1898. *The Romance of a Plain Man* runs from 1875 to 1910. For the post-Construction years *Virginia* covers 1884 to 1912; *Life and Gabriella*, 1894 to 1912. *The Miller of Old Church* starts in 1898 and closes in 1902; *Barren Ground* opens in 1894 and ends in 1924. *The Sheltered Life* goes from 1910 to 1917. *The Romantic Comedians* is compressed into the year 1923; *They Stooped to Folly*, into six months of 1924. *Vein of Iron* confines itself to the new century, 1901 to 1933, and *In This Our Life* concludes the social history by bringing the chronology up to 1939. According to this brief outline, Ellen Glasgow's novels, published between 1897 and 1941, exceed the seventy-one years of her lifetime, and supply an authentic record of social, political, and economic conditions in Virginia for about eighty-nine years. With the exception of *The Descendant*, *Phases of an Inferior Planet*, and *The Wheel of Life*, which used New

York City as setting, the novels are laid in various scenes of Virginia, usually the Tidewater district, Southside, or the Valley of Virginia.

The Commonwealth of Virginia reflected with particular sharpness the passing of the old and the coming of the new. Lethargy had never characterized her native sons. When their gracious mode of life was threatened from the North, they threw themselves first into the forensic battle to stem the pressure against their established institutions. The tide of change was relentless. Just as the South failed in its bloody fight against the industrial might of the Union, so did it lose ground in attempting to preserve its time-honored manner of life—an aristocracy supported by a slave population and a poor-white class, and devoted to the niceties of leisurely pursuits. The breakdown of a dominant aristocratic group sowed opportunities for a hitherto underprivileged class: the common man rose in the South to take his place in politics, education, wealth, and social recognition. The romantic glamour of plantation life gave way to the materialism and practicality of a new generation of thinkers and doers. Forms went out. Action came in. The current of life began to flow after threatened stagnation. Those so indoctrinated by tradition in the old manner of life could not change, and harked back to the past while surrounded by proof of the present.

All those indications of a changing civilization occupy the stage in Ellen Glasgow's novels. So also appear here in full stature the common men who respond to the long withheld challenge of education and opportunity. Her novels bring out another part of society, previously repressed and suppressed against full expression of individuality, talents, ability, and intellect. Almost any woman born into cultivated Southern society prior to the War Between the States was supposed to fulfill a designated role, as a dependent, acquiescent, ornamental appendage to the male. This check upon woman in the South aroused the author's concern, and stimulated her wit, irony, satire, and sympathy. On the other hand, she welcomed the impulse to freedom, where she saw it in a postbellum South, and illumined the heroic efforts of her heroines to carve their own careers, financially and spiritually, without the subjugating support or the dominating influence of the male.

A closer reading brings realization of the extent and depth with which Ellen Glasgow has achieved a social history of her section through the medium of the novel. The static quality of the romanticized Southern fiction is absent. Change in the old, gracious forms of living is anticipated. Actualities of war are exposed. The throes of Reconstruction overturn intrenched classes. In a reversal of political, economical, and social life a new class is identified, rising from their dim parlors into the sunlight and turbulence of new occupations. The modes and manners of an agrarian society yield to the pressure of industrialism.

Ellen Glasgow realized that she did not have to look afield for subject matter when she could see so much drama occurring in her own Virginia. Aware of its past glory, alert to its future strength, she admitted that inevitability of change, and urged her countrymen to discard shams of the past, and, with truth, energy, and courage, to adopt a realistic approach to the present. The result would seem to be a most complete running commentary of the defeat and rise of the South as personified in one state. Such a cycle has universal implications, but for Americans, especially historians, particular interest lies in her creation of a social record of these crucial years in all her novels.

NOTES

1. Description of Dinwiddie in *Virginia*, 13.
2. Frederic Taber Cooper, "Representative American Story Tellers: Ellen Glasgow," *Bookman*, XXIX (August 1909), 613.
3. Joyce Kilmer, "Evasive Idealism in Literature: Ellen Glasgow," *Literature in the Making* (New York: Harper, 1917), 232.
4. James Branch Cabell, *Some of Us, an Essay in Epitaphs* (New York: Robert M. McBride, 1930), 51.
5. James Branch Cabell, "Two Sides of the Shielded," *New York Herald Tribune Books*, April 20, 1930, 11.

6. H. L. Mencken, "A Southern Skeptic," *The American Mercury*, August 1933, 506.
7. Dorothea Lawrance Mann, "Ellen Glasgow: Citizen of the World," *Bookman*, LXIV (November 1926), 270.
8. Henry Seidel Canby, "Ellen Glasgow: Ironic Tragedian," *The Saturday Review of Literature*, XVIII (September 10, 1938), 14.
9. Douglas Southall Freeman, "Ellen Glasgow: Idealist," *The Saturday Review of Literature*, XII (August 31, 1935), 12.
10. Nellie Elizabeth Monroe, *A Critical Study of the Modern Novel* (Chapel Hill: University of North Carolina Press, 1941), 167.
11. Nellie Elizabeth Monroe, *A Critical Study of the Modern Novel* (Chapel Hill: University of North Carolina Press, 1941), 168.

II
Her Life

To obtain the facts in the life of Ellen Glasgow, we can consult biographical dictionaries, periodicals, and obituaries at the time of her death, November 21, 1945. *A Certain Measure*, which made available in 1943 a collection of prefaces to the Old Dominion Edition, tells much about her thought, method, and work. The appearance in 1954 of her autobiography, *The Woman Within*, and, in 1958, her *Letters* provide the best opportunity for understanding this artist.[1]

No startling events signified that Ellen Glasgow would take to letters, and join the front rank of American novelists. She was supposedly destined by delicate health to lead a quiet, secluded existence, without formal schooling. Her active mind, however, made small allowance for a frail constitution, and drove her to early browsing in her father's well-stocked library in the home on the corner of West Main and Foushee Streets, Richmond. She learned the alphabet from a novel of Scott's, under the tutelage of her mother or her Aunt Rebecca.

She began to write earlier than most authors. At the age of seven she concocted "A Lonely Daisy in a Field of Roses," later wilfully destroyed as was *Sharp Realities*, written at sixteen.

Browning she found for herself at thirteen. Three years later she enjoyed the influence of a brilliant young teacher of political economy, whose early death did not come before he had instilled in his pupil an interest in socialism, economics, and politics. History, literature, economics, and philosophy occupied a large part of her reading, especially authors such as Tolstoi (*War and Peace*), Dostoevski, Richardson, Fielding, Sterne, Swift, Maupassant, Flaubert, Hardy, Austen, Proust, Voltaire, and Darwin.[2] In an interview with Robert Van Gelder, she asserted that no other writer influenced her in any direct way.[3] Certainly she never imitates; her thought and expression are instinctively her own.

Ellen Glasgow's roots went back to Revolutionary forebears, and included a Scotch-Irish strain. On her father's side, educators and lawyers had distinguished the family. Her father had managed the local iron foundry, which had supplied most of the heavy caliber cannon to the Confederacy.

Among the ten children of Francis Thomas and Anne Jane Gholson Glasgow, Ellen, born April 22, 1874, was ninth. When she was twelve, the family acquired the large, square, gray brick house at 1 West Main Street, built about 1825. Surrounded by an iron fence, this colonial home, with its square porch and two columns, with its garden at the rear and its large study on the second floor front, provided the author's peaceful retreat for contemplation and writing, and served as setting for all her composition except for *Life and Gabriella*, which was written in New York. In Richmond Miss Glasgow passed all her seventy-one years except for nearly a year in New York, excursions to Italy, Germany, and England, and summers late in life at Castine, Maine.

To Richmond came distinguished friends: Mary Johnston, May Sinclair, Burton Rascoe, Princess Troubetzkoy, Douglas Southall Freeman, Joseph Hergesheimer, Hugh Walpole, Arnold Bennett, James Branch Cabell, William Allen White, and others to enjoy dignified and stimulating conversation, which Miss Glasgow's slight deafness scarcely retarded. Their impressions create for us a lovely person, with eloquent dark eyes, and beautiful bronze hair.

Around her were generally one or two pet dogs; the most famous, a poodle and a sealyham named Jeremy. Her love of animals and hatred of suffering impelled her to establish the Richmond Society for the Prevention of Cruelty to Animals, and to direct it, as president, for many years. She pursued the hobby of collecting porcelain and pottery dogs, and, upon her death, left a collection of seventy-five to the Valentine Museum, Richmond. Golf figured as another hobby, and her game has been described as "good."

There runs throughout her novels a rebellious voice against the social situation of women. In action, she was rarely militant in her attitude for women's rights. Yet, she did participate in a suffrage parade on May 4, 1912, in New York City, and already had led a character through a similar experience—Aunt Matoaca Bland in *The Romance of a Plain Man,* published in 1909. Her friends in Richmond's Association Opposed to Woman Suffrage found such conduct hard to reconcile with conduct becoming a lady.

These known biographical facts offer slim bases for Ellen Glasgow's break with tradition, critical view of Southern civilization, and realistic awareness of facts. Her theories were certainly ahead of the times, and in opposition to Southern conventions. We accept the anomaly gratefully. Her novels were influential in the emancipation of modern woman, and, if they did not hew the way with an axe, they certainly marked it with a rapier.

NOTES

1. Ellen Glasgow, *The Woman Within* (New York: Harcourt, Brace and Company, 1954).

   Ellen Glasgow, *Letters,* comp. by Blair Rouse (New York: Harcourt, Brace and Company, 1958).

   Ellen Glasgow, "Jordan's End": story with biographical note, *Scholastic,* XL (January 22, 1945), 21-22.

   Fred B. Millett, *Contemporary American Authors* (New York: Harcourt, Brace and Company, 1940), 374.

   Grant M. Overton, "Ellen Glasgow's Arrow," *Bookman,* LX (May 1925), 291-96.

   Publishers' Weekly, CXLVIII (December 1, 1945), 2448.

   Eudora Ramsay Richardson, "Richmond and Its Writers," *Bookman,* LXVIII (December 1928), 449-53.

   Time, XXXVII (March 31, 1941), 71-74.

Alice M. Tyler, "Ellen Glasgow: Her Books and Her Personality," *Book News*, XXX (August 1912), 843-48.

Who's Who in America, 1946-47, XXIV (1947), 878-79.

Wilson Library Bulletin, IV (May 1930), 424, XX (January 1946), 328.

2. Nellie Elizabeth Monroe, *The Novel and Society* (Chapel Hill: University of North Carolina Press, 1941), 149-50.

3. Robert Van Gelder, *Writers and Writing* (Scribner, 1946), 321 (reprint from *New York Times Book Review*, October 18, 1942).

III

The Literary and
Social Backgrounds
of the Novels

There never seems to have been any question in the mind of this writer where to go for material. Ellen Glasgow said she wrote about Virginia, because that was the locale which she knew best. An earlier literalness on details of place and persons dovetailed, through greater experience and understanding, into truthful interpretations of life, without rigid, factual treatment. She undoubtedly drew characters, actions, and speech partly from surrounding types. She, herself, refuted numerous claims of Richmond citizens to recognize themselves or their relatives in her characters. In her own words, "But I have not ever, I repeat, borrowed wholly from life."[1] And, "Although I have not ever tried to draw a complete portrait from life, finding that exact copies of human beings invariably fade and die in one's hands, I have, now and then, filled in an outline by piecing fragments together."[2] Imagination, plus close observation, is responsible for her convincing characterizations.

Evasive idealism was one of the last illusions of the South to go. Concentrating upon the gentlewoman, it fed on the supposition, says Ellen Glasgow, that "the Southern belle and beauty was still a recognized ornament to society. As an emblem, she followed closely the mid-Victorian ideal, and though her sort was found everywhere in the Western world, it was in Virginia that she seemed to attain her finest and latest flowering."[3] Although the gentlewoman has existed, more or less precariously, in all parts of the world, the native climate and soil of the

South have combined with its particular institutions to furnish for her species an appropriate background of fauna and flora."[4]

Amanda Lightfoot, the "pattern of pure womanhood," in *The Romantic Comedians,* knew the "severe discipline of the great tradition."[5] She spent a lifetime molding herself according to the sentimental, theoretical tastes of Judge Gamaliel Bland Honeywell, only to be passed over, when the widowed Judge sought a new helpmeet, in favor of her direct opposite, a modern, young, golddigger. *The Deliverance* does more than draw a portrait of a Southern gentlewoman in Mrs. Blake. Blind, shielded by her impoverished family, she symbolizes the South which cannot change, but, deceived by its illusions, saps the strength of the next generation.

Although at her best with aristocratic types, Miss Glasgow does not confine herself to this stratum of society, for she knows that the entire social structure of the South is in process of revolution. While Christopher Blake spews venom over lost privileges and heritage, his family's former overseer, Fletcher, acquires the Blake plantation and rises to power. Whereas Christopher has been denied his rightful advantages and education, Maria Fletcher, through her father's change of fortune, has acquired breeding and polish. From this reversal of social standing and wealth, Miss Glasgow has developed almost a melodramatic, but credible, presentation of Reconstruction conditions.

In *The Voice of the People, The Romance of a Plain Man,* and *One Man in His Time* she was again occupied with the attractions of opposites, as lovers, on the social scale and proves the worth of the common people, given an opportunity to develop. Nicholas Burr, Ben Starr, and Gideon Vetch distinguish themselves in government and finance. The history of the South for this period, 1870 to 1910 inclusively, offers completely adequate substantiation. Railroads were penetrating this section, bringing contact with the outside world and offering scope for the energies and ambitions of the new businessman or railroad magnate. The lower social orders, awake to the need of reformed, enlightened legislation, successfully sent their representatives into state legislatures. To get the facts for *The Voice of the People,* published in 1900, Miss Glasgow journeyed to Roanoke, persuaded a friend to smuggle her into the Democratic party's state convention, where, for two hot August days, she ascertained actual conditions of political conventions. Needless to say, she was the only woman present, unseen and unheard.

Ellen Glasgow called herself a "rebel," one of the "disinherited," since she disagreed so boldly with customs imposed by her own aristocratic group. Another label easily attached is that of innovator. Polite literature in 1897 did not center upon a hero of dubious parentage (Michael Akershem in *The Descendant*). A young lady, scarcely twenty, was supposed to be unacquainted with the word "bastard." Before the term "miscegenation" had acquired current usage during the inflamed discussion of *Strange Fruit* up Boston way, she had brought out *Virginia* in 1913, which, in a few, vivid flashes, exposes Cyrus Treadwell's relationship to Mandy, the colored washwoman, and, in 1932, *The Sheltered Life*, which had painted quite definitely and unhesitatingly George Birdsong's affair with Memoria, the mulatto. Miss Glasgow not only depicted the pitiable plight of fallen women in her time, but picked them up and set them on their feet again, in defiance of all convention that the woman should pay and pay. "For once, in Southern fiction, the betrayed woman would become the victor instead of the victim."[6]

These spot notations give some indication of the varieties of types to be found in her novels, and their departures from current practice. Gone are the romantic heroes of antebellum days and the radiant, helpless women they pursue adoringly. The woman gives a hearty boot to her pedestal, acquires the feel of solid ground under her feet, and demonstrates, in action, the vitality of blood coursing through her veins.

No character in these novels exists in an isolated vacuum. The author's philosophy expresses itself on this point succinctly, when in *A Certain Measure* she states:

> Though the chief end of the novel is to create life, there is a secondary obligation which demands that fiction shall, in a measure at least, reflect the movement and the tone of its age.[7]

Deliberately, then, the personal plot or conflict is laid against a background or setting veritably functional in its participation. Dorinda Oakley, as woman farmer in the isolated, impoverished, broomsedge area of Virginia, which *Barren Ground* utilizes, represents a human being's mastery of an unfriendly fortune, symbolizes the rise of the new South against hostile conditions of the postwar era—against poverty, poor soil, loneliness, lack of education and opportunity.

From these novels may be constructed a very adequate version of the times in Virginia. For all its youthful tendency to romanticism, *The Battle-Ground* underscores the futilities of existence in life on the plantations for women like Betty Ambler and Mrs. Lightfoot, capable of better things, or at least more mental than their lot in life prescribes. It emphasizes the impact of realistic warfare, which smears blood over glory and denotes the utter bewilderment and destitution of the privileged classes at the close of the war. *The Deliverance* pictures the breakdown of the old order, the passing of property and control into the hands of unscrupulous newcomers among the whites, and captures the bitterness and maladjustment of Reconstruction turmoil. *The Voice of the People* salutes the new average man of the people, who, by sheer determination and tenacity, elevates himself to a position of leadership in government, and there, through basic good sense and principle, achieves much for the general welfare.

The fiction of Ellen Glasgow is faithful to historical perspective. *The Romance of a Plain Man* narrates how General Bolingbroke, a member of the old prominent regime, directs his energy and intelligence into the realms of finance and railroad expansion after the war, and then, in advanced years, relinquishes the reins of power to Ben Starr, a new, ambitious arrival on the scene.

The Miller of Old Church cites another instance where an enterprising, industrious hero from the ranks raises himself by his bootstraps to prosperity in material goods and authority in state government. These individual cases bear out the author's thesis that the introduction of new blood to supplant the old

was accomplishing diversified representation in the affairs of
the South, was providing the white classes, for the first time,
with democracy, in fact as well as in theory. Salvation for the
South lay in her adaptation to new conditions, to broadened
communication and transportation, to the establishment of mills,
to modernized agricultural methods, and to expanded markets
by the concomitant of free labor. Feudalism, sectionalism, and
isolation had to give way to broader contacts with the rest of
the country and the rest of the world. Predominantly agricultural, even in 1898, with cotton and tobacco still the staple
products, Virginia made way for industrialization.

Just as money infiltrated from the North for investment in
railroad and mill building, it found its way into the establishment and improvement of educational facilities, in a program
chiefly sponsored by denominational groups. The South, on the
whole, had made creditable beginnings in the higher education
of women. Among colleges open to women, established in the
United States prior to the war, were the Elizabeth Female
Seminary, founded at Washington, Mississippi, in 1818; the Mississippi College, a coeducational institution at Clinton, in 1830;
and the Georgia Female College, now known as Wesleyan
College, which the State of Georgia chartered in 1836 and which
was the first college for women to give the A.B. Mary Sharp
College started at Winchester, Tennessee, in 1850, under the
name Tennessee and Alabama Female Institute, but died in the
eighties.

The Old Dominion lagged, however, in the field of female
education until 1852 when the Hollins Female Institute, now
Hollins College, opened near Roanoke. In the eighties, the
South boasted 145 institutions of higher learning for women, in
contrast with the North's 111, and in 1882 the South conferred
684 degrees upon women, whereas the North issued only 220.
In spite of quantity, however, the South did not equal the
quality of instruction which Northern colleges for women, such
as Vassar, Wellesley, and Smith, were dispensing.[8] The romantic
notions that had colored indelibly every phase of antebellum
life and had hindered progress in the emancipation of woman

yielded perceptibly to the influx of postwar demands. A few men dissented with the inferior instruction prevailing for women. Walter Hines Page spoke in 1897 on the subject of "The Forgotten Woman," in an endeavor to stimulate sympathy for educational opportunity of women below the Mason and Dixon Line.[9]

Advance in educational and economic matters emanated, to some degree, from a new spirit of nationalism in America that was being fostered by writers of both the North and South. Unlike rabid politicians who capitalized on the old friction between sections, unlike the Republicans who kept themselves in power by prolonged waving of "the bloody shirt," authors made haste soon after the Reconstruction period to sound the notes of reconciliation. Magazines like *Scribner's* (later named *The Century*), *The Atlantic Monthly*, *Lippincott's*, even *Harper's* by the middle eighties, and more popular magazines like *The Cosmopolitan*, *Munsey's* and *McClure's* devoted many pages and issues to Southern themes in a sympathetic vein. These periodicals gave space not only to Southern talent on Southern topics —Joel Chandler Harris, Thomas Nelson Page, Walter Hines Page, James Lane Allen, George W. Cable, Mary Noailles Murfree, Maurice Thompson, Sidney Lanier, and Mary Johnston— but to a coterie of Northerners who likewise employed Southern settings—Frank R. Stockton, Sarah Orne Jewett, Thomas Bailey Aldrich, Bret Harte, Robert Chambers, and others.[10]

The theater, too, drenched itself in the romantic idealism of the Southern past—the benevolent, mint julep-drinking colonel, devotedly attended by an old Negro servant on the porch of the columned plantation home. Between 1886 and 1900, William Gillette's *Held by the Enemy*, Bronson Howard's *Shenandoah*, David Belasco's *The Girl I Left Behind Me*, James A. Herne's *Griffith Davenport*, and Clyde Fitch's *Barbara Frietchie* catered to the popular taste, which throve on this romantic fare, and reminisced upon the South's former glory with heavy sentiment.[11]

These literary eulogies of a defeated people undoubtedly promoted better feeling between the victor and the vanquished, softened the temper of the first and palliated the resentment of the second, but, as so often happens with good things, they lost essential moderation and proportion. The legend of a heroic past persisted in constantly magnified form. Nostalgia glossed the Confederacy with greater beauty and perfection than it had ever possessed, as it receded more and more into affectionate memory, until, for those inimical to, or incapable of, change, it acquired veritably the sanctity of a religion. Conveniently forgotten were the abominations connected with a slave-holding order. The romance, only, lingered in recollection.

Ellen Glasgow declined to play on this repetitive motif. Frankly she singled out the evils, the inconsistencies, the fallacies, and the weaknesses of this ingrowing conception of the South, and decried in *Virginia, Life and Gabriella, The Romantic Comedians, They Stooped to Folly,* and *The Sheltered Life* the harmful consequences that this grave misconception of reality had generated. The statuesque woman who was being idealized beyond normality in the glorification of a Southern history, who was obliged to get along without mental stimuli, financial independence, or political participation aroused the author to sympathize and to revolt.

The protest against the social status of woman involved a stand against the state of mind so prevalent in her section, a condition which Ellen Glasgow termed "evasive idealism." Through the lines or behavior of her characters, she attacked the attitude, based upon sentimentalism, that blindly ignored the presence of ugliness: the attitude that leaned toward looking on the bright side of life, that preferred to cling to a dream world of tradition rather than to face the problems of the immediate present, that trusted in an antiquity on the sheer basis of its age, that let the world go by from simple inertia, that could not admit the urgency of the moment's challenge. Healthy optimism she did advocate, but not the kind of narrow optimism that avoided reality, that fed upon illusions. The inability or unwillingness of some Southerners to deal with political, social, and economic ills afflicting their section oppressed her.

The balance of power between the two sexes elicited satirical comment. She deplored the elevation of woman to a pedestal which curtailed her ability to feel, to think, or to act, which served only the primary requisite of satisfying the vanity of man in his invention of the "womanly woman." Miss Glasgow took mischievous delight in destroying man's reliance upon evasive idealism to explain his relationship to the weaker sex, his complacency over her sacrifice to his ego, and his hypocrisy, disclosed by the discrepancy between theory and action. She opposed vigorously, wherever and whenever she found them, cruelty, ugliness, hypocrisy, sentimentalism, and false optimism.

Joyce Kilmer thought of her as an optimist, not a sentimental optimist, but a protagonist of a robust, genuine optimism. Her novels, even at their darkest, as in the case of *Barren Ground* and *Vein of Iron*, affirm the will to live, assert that there is meaning in life that warrants and justifies the effort of the struggles. Especially did Miss Glasgow manifest a keen realization of the plight of woman prevented from living fully by the attentions of her male protector. She voices repeatedly the woman's right to live her own life independently of her relationship to man, and to piece together again an acceptable life after his defection. This latter theme motivates *Life and Gabriella, Barren Ground*, and *Vein of Iron*, where the deserted women recreate for themselves new lives after disastrous experiences with lovers.

Insofar as she enunciated intellectual, social, and economic heresies through her heroines, Ellen Glasgow could be called a feminist of a radical hue. Her own definition for feminism supplies a key:

> Feminism is a revolt from pretense of being—it is, at its best and worst, a struggle for the liberation of personality.[12]

NOTES

1. Ellen Glasgow, *A Certain Measure* (New York: Harcourt, Brace, and Company, 1943), 217.
2. *Ibid.*, 161.
3. *Ibid.*, 45.

4. *Ibid.*, 78.
5. *The Romantic Comedians*, 218.
6. Ellen Glasgow, *A Certain Measure*, 24.
7. *Ibid.*
8. Virginius Dabney, *Liberalism in the South* (Chapel Hill: University of North Carolina Press, 1932), 365-68.
9. *Ibid.*, 369-70.
10. Paul H. Buck, *The Road to Reunion*, 1865-1900 (Boston: Little, Brown, and Company, 1937), 221-27, 196-219.
11. *Ibid.*, 233.
12. Ellen Glasgow, "Feminism, a Definition," *Good Housekeeping,* LVIII (May 1914), 683.

IV

A Realist Looks
at the South

By now the notion of any "Ivory Tower" in connection with Ellen Glasgow is farthest from our thoughts. Yet, we feel some curiosity over the distance intervening between her outlook and that from an Ivory Tower. Her realism, which elicited denunciations from pulpits at the turn of the century, strikes us now, more than forty years later, as still deserving the name. In one aspect, only, it differs from the modern school, because it never deviates from the criterion of good taste or the standards of literary excellence.

Her realism depended upon the method of seeing things clearly, reporting them truthfully, and exposing them critically. Her "realism" . . . is the penetration of pretense," says Emily Clark.[1] "She is disillusioned without being disappointed," adds Margaret Lawrence.[2] She belongs, agrees Harlan Hatcher, among "the first realists at the turn of the century."[3] According to Donald Adams, she has endowed many of her heroines with this penetrating insight: "And yet, with few exceptions, her women are the realists."[4]

Illegitimate babies abound in these novels. Heroines like Gabriella, Dorinda, and Ada do not even satisfy the romantic standards for beauty and charm. They start in youth, but progress to middle age before reaching the conclusions of their stories.[5] All three bid farewell to the romantic illusions of youth. Gabriella actually flees in middle age from the honorable intentions of a life-long admirer, a typical Southern gentleman of the old school. Practicality, resourcefulness, industry, and courage—

the strength to confront facts and to rationalize—sever these women from their counterparts in contemporary romantic fiction.

Ellen Glasgow apparently aimed at realism at the very start of her career. She claimed that *"The Voice of the People* was the first work of genuine realism to appear in Southern fiction."[6] Certainly many of its details had a down-to-earth appeal. The carrot-topped, freckled-faced, awkward lad, Nicholas Burr, son of the ineffectual peanut farmer, boasted of none of the romantic features or promising characteristics of conventional heroes.

If readers had understood the subtle *Virginia* correctly when it was first published in 1913, they would have appreciated better its domestic realism; they would have perceived in this tragi-comedy of manners a biting criticism of prevailing family conventions and a denunciation of useless, feminine self-sacrifice. *Barren Ground,* published in 1925, accented with tragic impressiveness the author's vital sense of realism. Readers were permanently enlightened as to her capacity for realism. Critics hastened to acclaim it for this very quality, for its almost brutal adherence to truth and reality in the details of characterization, setting, and plot.

Miss Glasgow's own statement aligns her in the vanguard of American realists, where she served a unique purpose in

> a solitary revolt against the formal, the false, the affected, the sentimental, and the pretentious in southern writing.[7]

> The true realists, I felt, must illuminate experience, not merely transcribe it; and so, for my own purpose, I defined the art of fiction as experience illuminated.[8]

The "art of fiction," which was a favorite term of hers for novel-writing, escaped under her manipulations the bonds of stereotyped romanticism, abandoned the tinge of idealism in *The Battle-Ground,* and, in *Barren Ground* and other works subsequent to *The Miller of Old Church,* forged ahead into the new school of modern realism.

Only a clear-eyed realist would have dared to reveal the emptiness of life for women encircled by taboos, to condemn a social system that enslaved not only a whole sex, but a whole race:

> In the old South this inherited culture possessed grace and beauty and the inspiration of gaiety. Yet it was shallow-rooted at best, since, for all its charm and its good will, the way of living depended, not upon its own creative strength, but upon the enforced servitude of an alien race. Not the fortunes of war, not the moral order of the universe, but economic necessity doomed the South to defeat.[9]

These quotations from *A Certain Measure* show the author's knack of seeing things as they really are. She analyzed the fundamental basis for evils in society, and, in many studies, delineated a positive philosophy dependent on courage, which can assure human beings of creative and dynamic qualities. The realism of Ellen Glasgow included disenchantment without despair, and vision without idealism.

NOTES

1. Emily Clark, *Innocence Abroad* (New York: Alfred Knopf, 1931), 66.
2. Margaret Lawrence, *School of Femininity* (New York: Frederick Stokes, 1936), 292-93.
3. Harlan Henthorne Hatcher, *Creating the Modern American Novel* (New York: Farrar and Rinehart, 1935), 95.
4. James Donald Adams, *The Shape of Books to Come* (New York: Viking Press, 1944), 119.
5. *Life and Gabriella, Barren Ground, Vein of Iron.*
6. James Southall Wilson, "Ellen Glasgow, Ironic Idealist," *Virginia Quarterly Review*, XV (January 1939), 123.
7. Ellen Glasgow, *A Certain Measure*, 8.
8. *Ibid.*, 14.
9. *Ibid.*, 13.

V

Categories

In the nineteenth century and the early part of the twentieth the South decreed a rigid code of conduct and thought for women. By burlesque and satire Ellen Glasgow attacked all the rules of the code, and thereby achieved a historical portrait of woman. The stature of woman, old style, before it expired in the 1920s, is of primary importance in *Virginia, They Stooped to Folly, The Sheltered Life,* and *The Romantic Comedians,* where the now extinct genre of heroine goes through excruciating trials and tribulations in conformity to custom. Being a modern, however, the author did not confine herself to this trusting sample of womanhood, but moved on to more enlightened and energized types in the liberated heroines of *Life and Gabriella, Barren Ground,* and *Vein of Iron.*

Ellen Glasgow dealt principally with two classes of society, in her social history of Virginia: the good families, living on the coast; and the good people, either the Scotch-Irish in the Valley of Virginia or the Anglo-Saxon stock in Southside. The first is, historically, more familiar to us, having been exploited for our entertainment in the fiction and drama of several generations.

The celebrated Southern beauty had one aim in life, to satisfy the ideal of the Southern gentleman and to cope with the tenor of a civilization for which he was largely responsible. She was typed according to circumstances and may, therefore, be viewed in the light of certain categories—the homemaker, or helpmeet; the frustrated spinster; the gay, sophisticated lady; the "perpetual widow"; and the rare careerist. Scattered among these were the shielded ladies; the innocent ladies whose shields had disintegrated; the ambitious, maternal ladies; the dependent relatives, married or single, useful or parasitic; and the thronging gallery of "fallen women."

As a helpmeet, Mrs. Ambler, in *The Battle-Ground*, evinces wifely humility toward her husband, the former governor, when she takes up "her work-box with a laugh of protest:

> "I am quite content with the mission of my sex, sir . . . I'm sure I'd much rather make shirt fronts for you than wear them myself."[1]

Both sexes seem to be blind to the actual state of affairs—that while the gentlemen read in the library or discuss politics there with neighbors over a bottle of wine, the women are busily occupied with administering huge plantations, running the households, providing for the meals, caring for the health and maintenance of slaves, and generally supervising things from morning until night. The resourcefulness of these ladies afford the means to cope with scarcities and other problems imposed by the war. During the absence of the men at the "Front," women's important services to their households become appreciated. Betty Ambler and Mrs. Lightfoot somehow care for the bewildered, freed slaves on their plantations, forage for food, and inspire renewed courage in the men after Appomattox.

The portraits of wives and mothers among the homemakers are consistently sympathetic. Mrs. Littlepage of *They Stooped to Folly* may not always think things through clearly, but as her nonconforming brother-in-law, Marmaduke, discerns, she invariably does the right thing. She visits the doleful Mrs. Burden in a vain effort to cheer that woman's lugubrious spirits; she administers charities, especially the "Home for Unfortunates," newly christened the "House of Hope." She shows tolerance toward her flighty son-in-law and domineering daughter. She comports herself, as a perfect wife should, throughout many married years, and conceals with fortitude impaired health and dwindling strength. She is a model wife and mother whose only defect, in the eyes of her husband, is the apparent absence of any human frailties.

Slightly shaded from this portrait appears that of the Rector's wife in *Virginia*. Mrs. Pendleton is driven by a consuming necessity for self-sacrifice and service. She will scrub floors, but she takes the precaution of tackling this demeaning task only at the crack of dawn, when her family will not be on hand to remonstrate. Her daughter, protagonist of the novel, arouses almost painful reactions in the reader. Inculcating the most admired features, this Southern flower blooms for only a short time in her virgin girlhood, long enough to cast a radiant spell over the young, intellectual Oliver Treadwell. The marriage proves to be misery for them both. She is incapable of sharing his thoughts and aspirations. When he reads his play to her, he is disappointedly conscious of her inattention, her posture of waiting for the baby's cry, her inability to accompany him out of the realm of domesticity. She is hurt repeatedly by his abstractions, becomes gradually aware that he is seeking solace in more stimulating feminine company elsewhere; yet, when she has a chance to face the situation and perhaps to work out some solution to their dilemma, she crumples at the prospect of unpleasantness and takes refuge in the worn mantle of pride. She retreats even more into concerns of the home, magnifying their importance, until, finally, she has lost touch with the outside interests of husband and children. Her beauty and vitality fade swiftly and are permanently blighted when Oliver desperately resorts to a divorce to end a hollow marriage. The beautiful girl who seemed cut out for happiness reaches middle age without a prop to lean on, deprived of domestic responsibilities, devoid of mental resources, and unequipped by endowment or training to deal with unexpected and disagreeable issues.

Another species of unhappy wife spends years in maintaining a pretense of a happy marriage. Of course Eva Birdsong's brave front convinces none that her union with George is satisfactory, but only incites further speculation whether or not she really knows of his flagrant infidelities. Her martyrdom breaks off abruptly when she kills George, bent on the seduction of a young neighbor. Eva, like Virginia, seemed destined for happiness, and, carried away by emotion, puts all her hopes for the future in a marriage based solely upon romantic impulse. She pays for her innocence and ignorance by bondage to a notorious philanderer. She has avoided reality too long to devise a reasonable escape from her predicament, unwilling to admit his unfaithfulness or to resort to divorce. Adherence to an idealistic code precludes any sane, sensible denouement to Eva's predicament, and prepares the way for the violent climax. Virginia and Eva, cast in destined roles as homemakers, fail to find security or serenity in marriage. Conditioned by their romantic dreams to expect everything from the holy state of wedlock, they are, unavoidably and tragically, victimized by their delusions. As products of an artificial civilization, they are striking examples of its inadequacies.

Loveless marriages occur abundantly as accidents of fate. Judge Honeywell, in *The Romantic Comedians*, was caught on the rebound of a lover's quarrel with Amanda Lightfoot by Cordelia, for whom he maintained only a passing fancy, and chivalrously supports the pretense of a happy marrage until Cordelia's death. In *The Sheltered Life*, General Archibald had the misfortune to compromise a young lady when his sleigh broke down; so, although his affections were engaged elsewhere and hers were directed to another man, he marries her with great gallantry. They dutifully maintain the semblance of a happy marriage, and stoically ignore the sacrifice of four lives to the gesture.

The second type of female in the social panorama of the South calls out Miss Glasgow's best display of wit and compassion. The frustrated spinster appeared to have been singled out by fate for a hard lot, which denied her any opportunity to express talent, which coerced her into a set pattern, and which thrust her, willingly or unwillingly, under the protection and authority of some male relative. Aunt Kesiah, in *The Miller of Old Church*, furnishes a conspicuous example of a promising woman born into the wrong age, born too soon to elude the clamps of destiny:

She was one of those unfortunate women of a past generation, who, in offering no allurement to the masculine eye, appeared to defeat the single end for which woman was formed. As her very right to existence lay in her possible power to attract, the denial of that power by nature, or the frustration of it by circumstances, had deprived her, almost from the cradle, of her only authoritative reason for being.[2]

In the words of her sister, Mrs. Gay:

"Once she got in a temper, and walked a mile or two in the road, but when she returned I was in such a state of nervousness that she promised me never to leave the lawn again, unless a gentleman was with her."[3]

Kesiah's ambition to paint drew this comment from Uncle William Burwell:

"Why on earth should a girl want to go streaking across the water to study art, when she had a home she could stay in and men folk who could look after her?"[4]

At any rate, Kesiah submitted to her family's judgment, discarded her yearning for art, and conformed to the life of a frustrated spinster who had an additional burden to bear in the domination of the insidiously sweet sister, Mrs. Gay, whose strength lay in her surface frailty:

She spoke in a sweet, helpless voice, and this helplessness was expressed in every lovely line of her figure. The most casual observer would have discerned that she dominated not by force, but by sentiment, that she had surrendered all rights in order to grasp more effectively at all privileges.[5]

The introduction to Kesiah, in the words of the author, sets a contrast:

It was the habit of those about her to forget her existence, except when she was needed to render service, and after more than fifty years of such omissions, she had ceased, even in her thoughts, to pass judgment upon them. In her youth she rebelled fiercely—

rebelled against nature, against the universe, against the fundamental injustice that divided her sister's lot from her own. Generations of ancestors had bred in her the belief that woman existed only to win love or to bestow it. Inheritance, training, temperament, all combined to develop the racial instinct within her, yet something stronger than these—some external shaping of clay—had unfitted her for the purpose for which she was designed. And since, in the eyes of her generation, any self-expression from a woman, which was not associated with sex, was an affront to convention, that single gift of hers was doomed to wither away in the hothouse air that surrounded her.[6]

In a few words on the portrait of Aunt Kesiah, the author compressed all the pathos inherent in the lives of frustrated, unmarried women misfits for the time and place.

The character Miss Danton escapes, rather tardily, the meshes that had thwarted Kesiah:

As a young girl, aflame with temperament, she had sacrificed herself to a widowed father and a family of little brothers and sisters in a small town in the South. For thirty years she had fought down her dreams and impulses; for thirty years she had cooked, washed, ironed, and sewed, until the children had all grown up and married, and her father, after a long illness, had died in her arms. On her fifty-second birthday her freedom had come—freedom not only from cares and responsibilities, but from love, from duty, from the constant daily thought that she was necessary to some one who depended on her. At fifty-three, with broken health and a few thousand dollars brought from the sale of the old home, she had come to New York to study music as she had dreamed of doing when she was young. And the tragedy of it was that she had a gift, she had temperament, she had genuine artistic feeling.[7]

There is no irony, only sympathy, in these descriptions of potential artists, whose creative spark was extinguished by drudgery, rather than fanned by opportunity, drudgery under the yoke of oppressive tradition. The attitude of the South, which fostered these sacrifices among talented women by curtailing their fields of endeavor and by encouraging their financial dependence, incurred Miss Glasgow's indignation.

While Aunt Etta droops from chronic ill health, while Aunt Kesiah substitutes household chores for art, while Aunt Lydia pokes away at her Chericoke garden, the mouselike Aunt Matoaca startles and scandalizes the good families of Richmond by tentative ventures into the cause for women's rights.[8] She reads the *verboten* political items in the newspaper, to the horror of her rejected suitor, General Bolingbroke, who would far rather see her more suitably occupied with cookbooks or the Bible. She stirs further censure by zealously distributing suffrage pamphlets and by marching prominently in a suffrage parade. She is a timid soul at best, who comes out from her ladylike retirement only under stress of a powerful feeling that her kind should be allowed political representation.

It is not surprising that her reasoning can go only part of the way in embracing the theories of women's rights, and stops short of aiming at complete, political freedom, for she "would prefer to have only 'ladies' permitted to vote."[9] She was yet a "slave of ancestry of men who oppressed women, and women who loved oppression."[10] What is significant is the articulation of any sort of political philosophy by the Aunt Matoacas, who contradicted so unexpectedly their inherited beliefs. These modest spinsters were not only decorating the Southern landscape, but applying to it some good, sound spade work that would uproot false doctrines and plant fresh, progressive ideas. Frustrated in their time, they will find honor later.

The next generation from Aunt Matoaca, represented in her niece, Sally Mickleborough, comes to the conclusion that "women must have larger lives—that they mustn't be expected to feed always upon their hearts."[11] The author proved, through poignant examples, that there existed no justification for restricting women to the home, that they deserved wider horizons according to their several necessities and abilities, and that unhappy wives and frustrated spinsters supplied ample cause for reproach in a so-called civilization.

For variations on a theme, Miss Glasgow did full justice to a gallery of gay, sophisticated ladies—introducing creatures once gay, but not sophisticated, ladies gay and sophisticated, and some sophisticated, but not gay. Her collection of fallen women generally fits into one or another description, perhaps with less emphasis on the gay except for the egregious case of Mrs. Dalrymple. Never had the situation of fallen woman been transcribed in literature with greater insight or truer fidelity or better skill than by Ellen Glasgow, who observed it minutely in the midst of Southern society.

The fallen women in her novels run the gamut from betrayed innocence to uninhibited worldliness. Isabella Archibald in *The Sheltered Life* has been caught in a predicament similar to her father's youthful one but, unfortunately, with a less honorable partner. As a consequence of her indiscretion, she has lost her value in the marriage market, if not her innocence, and is shunned by seriously intentioned suitors. In *They Stooped to Folly*, a more impressive retribution in the wages of sin haunts Aunt Agatha, whose girlish trust in a man precipitated a shocking scandal for the digestion of Queensborough. For her capitulation Aunt Agatha paid with the best years of her life, living submissively in a third-floor back room at the Littlepages, and preserving, according to the finest tradition, the anonymity of her betrayer, although persistent conjecture of interested parties was strongly inclined toward the gay figure of Colonel Bletheram, who during an active life "had lost three faithful wives but never missed a Christmas cotillion."[12] Aunt Agatha's baby was spirited away with a celerity that only the need for drastic action in the face of dire necessity contrives. Aunt Agatha wears her invisible scarlet letter with commendable humility, and leads the life of a recluse, immured in her tiny room, from which she creeps at meal time only if the immediate family is present. At the dinner table she never initiates a remark, but is never totally ignored, for "even when they were small, Victoria [Mrs. Littlepage] had exacted that the children should address at least one cheerful remark to poor Aunt Agatha at every meal."[13]

Virginian society, in prescribing this discreet formula of conduct for such deplorable situations as Aunt Agatha's, reckoned without allowance for the catalytic agency of war, and was obliged to sit idly by while abnormal conditions of a war at-

mosphere made inroads on its cherished code of behavior. Among
the first to benefit from the lowered standards of morals is Aunt
Agatha, who emerges somewhat hesitatingly from her cocoon
sheath to sew pajamas for the soldiers, and stumbles upon unexpected diversions by way of lurid moving pictures and rich
banana sundaes. For a companion to her newly discovered
amusements, Agatha turns to one Mrs. Dalrymple, a divorcee
of many accomplishments, who has returned to her old happy
hunting grounds in Queensborough after conspicuous conquests
in Europe, quite apart from her gallant war service.

Twelve years previously Amy Dalrymple exercised for Mr.
Littlepage an almost fatal fascination that brought him close to
the brink of marital infidelity, and now that she is again in
circulation in Queensborough, with the added glamour of a
war record, she allures him anew. He very nearly succumbs to
her now slightly shopworn sex attraction, and is saved not so
much by his legal judgment as by his faltering spirit. Mrs. Dalrymple's life traces a different pattern from Aunt Agatha's, being
one generation later. Far from subdued by the extent and in-
tensity of her numerous love affairs, Mrs. Dalrymple continues
her aggressions on the male front, using her tarnished attractions expertly and spiritedly. She still passes as a very gay lady.

It takes the third and youngest generation to put to rout the
decrepit superstition of the fallen woman. Milly Burden, Mr.
Littlepage's secretary, refuses to realize her position among the
disowned, or to look upon her unfortunate experience with
Martin Welding as a blight upon her life. She has no intentions
of molding her behavior in imitation of Aunt Agatha, and asserts
her creed defiantly to Mr. Littlepage:

> "I have a right to my own happiness as long as I play the
> game fairly."[14]

After Mary Victoria Littlepage extended her charity work in
the Balkans to include the person of Martin Welding, she decides
that she can most effectively be "a power for good"[15] in the
life of Milly Burden's former lover through marriage, which she

proceeds to engineer with dispatch and without the knowledge of her father. Judge Littlepage, crushed by the conviction that he was instrumental in diverting Martin from Milly to his daughter, and overwhelmed by remorse for Milly's despair, sadly reflects:

> "The truth is that the world has never been fair to women. Men have never been fair to women."[16]

That, for one of Mr. Littlepage's age, inheritance, and environment, shows an advanced point of view. In a later conversation with Milly Burden, he finds out, by questioning, what value she respects and searches for:

> "Is anything sacred to you, Milly?"
> "Truth would be, if I could find it. Truth that you could really believe in, not just shams and labels."[17]

An epilogue for this novel of the haunted woman the author assigned to the indomitable Aunt Louisa, a devoted, life-long friend of the family and a pillar of strength, who muses:

> Nothing was worth all the deceit, all the anguish, all the futile hope and ineffectual endeavor, all the pretense and parade, all the artificial glamour and empty posturing, of the great Victorian tradition. . . . She knew what it had meant to women. She had lived through the ages of waiting, and she knew every throb, every ache, every pang, and every quiver. She had lived through it all. For her heart had cracked and broken as quietly as the hearts of all perfect Southern ladies broke beneath the enamelled surface of beautiful behavior. And now, cool, composed, indulgent, self-contained, and easily amused, she watched with sympathy the liberal manners of a new century.[18]

The Romantic Comedians spins its web of comic episodes more mirthfully by use of contrast between the staid Judge Honeywell and his ebullient twin sister, Mrs. Bredalbane. The latter epitomizes the gay, sophisticated lady in her quest for new sensation, her relish in the moment, and her disregard of public opinion. Arriving back in Queensborough after a youth strenuously spent in pursuit of pleasure on the Continent, she finds a more tolerant reception on the part of her contemporaries, now that she is no longer dangerously seductive, and an admiring attentiveness on the part of a youthful generation, seeing her escapades in the light of a glamorous past. Edmonia Bredalbane has a flair for speaking the truth upon impulse, for giving vulgarity in speech free rein, and she jars the Judge's sensibilities frequently to the breaking point. In the words of the author she takes concrete shape:

> Large, raw-boned, with strong, plain features, where an expression of genuine humor frolicked with an artificial complexion, and a mountainous bosom, from which a cascade of crystal beads splashed and glistened, Mrs. Bredalbane billowed toward him, while he thought: "If only she would dress with the dignity suitable to her size and her mature years!"[19]

> She was immoderate; she was indecorous; she was reprehensible; yet, she was again, he felt, in some absurd and even sinister way unanswerable. . . . Her sinful past, for her many marriages had merely whitewashed it, had not saddened her, had not sobered her, had not even, he concluded, with his stern but just gaze on her broad and lumpy back, diminished her size. She had not only thriven, she had fattened on iniquity. At sixty-five, a time of life surely when bad women turn to remorse, and even good women find little to turn to but duty, she flaunted (there was no other word for it) she actually flaunted her brazen past.[20]

Thus, even in Virginia, where the flower of womanhood blossomed to highest perfection, there were the ladies of dubious reputation, both in and out of the best circles, and no social history could fail to take them into account. The Aunt Agathas, the Amy Dalrymples, the Milly Burdens, and the Edmonia Bredalbanes add zest, vitality, and meaning to Miss Glasgow's interrogation of the social situation of women. They stand out in relief against their more numerous, more dutiful, and less adventurous sisters in the South.

Included in the ranks of the latter are the "perpetual widows of the South,"[21] furnishing a diverting spectacle in feminine psychology. Widowhood adopts a solemn, prolonged condition, observed by outward show when the cause of dress and bearing has very likely been nearly forgotten. The dignified, enhancing symbols cling to the bereaved until such a time as a willing male appears to solace her. A "beautiful grief" obsesses Mrs. Carr in *Life and Gabriella*:

> But when he was once safely dead she worshipped his memory with an ardour which would have seemed to her indelicate had he been still alive. For sixteen years she had worn a crepe veil on her bonnet, and she still went occasionally, after the morning service was over on Sunday, to place fresh flowers on his grave. . . . For her daughters she had drawn an imaginary portrait of him which combined the pagan beauty of Antinous with the military purity of Saint Paul.[22]

A brief glimpse characterizes the "beautiful old lady, Mrs. Peyton":

> She never goes anywhere but to church or to the Old Ladies' Home . . . she hasn't paid a call since her husband's death.[23]

The widow Mrs. Upchurch presents a cheerful, although not overly optimistic, watchful waiting for the miracle of another husband, and is about to resign herself to oblivion and to concentrate on her daughter's prospects for marriage:

> Marriage, as she remembered it, was a wearing experience; and though she still besought Providence for a rich and indulgent husband for herself and father for her child, her prayers had become simply another monotonous ritual.[24]

This philosophical outlook fortifies her when her contemporary, Judge Honeywell, comes courting, not her hand, but her daughter's, and enables her to further the unsuitable match.

These sad ladies, stranded in the status of widowhood, wear out their lonely years, for the most part, by encasing the memory of the departed in an aura of scented romance. Or, like Mrs.

Upchurch, they follow the policy of watchful waiting. They are even less enviable than their neighbors in the social category.

Ellen Glasgow considers another female in this category, the rare careerist, and draws her convincingly. Social decorum permitted few sources of livelihood or self-expression to women of aristocratic lineage, whether or not they had male relatives upon whom they could lean for support. Neither ability nor economic necessity determined the occupations of these genteel specimens, but, instead, the outmoded customs of a lost generation dictated the direction of their efforts into three basic channels. The most respected demanded the least preparation and the least expenditure of energy, Miss Priscilla Batte decided:

> With the majority of maiden ladies left destitute in Dinwiddie after the war, she had turned naturally to teaching as the only nice and respectable occupation which required neither preparation of mind nor considerable outlay of money. The fact that she was the single surviving child of a gallant Confederate general . . . was sufficient recommendation in the eyes of her fellow-citizens.[25]

Teaching as a possibility for Gabriella finds favor with her Uncle Meriweather:

> "Yes, let her teach by all means. . . . I've always regarded teaching as an occupation that ought to be restricted by law to needy ladies."[26]

So, judged by contemporary standards, teaching demanded little and rewarded less, lacked the dignity or requirements of a profession, and attracted to its practice unqualified and indigent ladies. If Miss Batte had happened to have an inquiring mind or if Gabriella had aspired to teach, the combination, hindered by time and place, would still have been ineffective.

A second means of livelihood that would not detract too seriously from social position was running a boardinghouse. Mrs. Carr in *Life and Gabriella*, Mrs. Peachey in *Virginia*, Mrs. Burden in *They Stooped to Folly*, and Mrs. Upchurch in *The Romantic Comedians* engage in this remunerative toil. Mrs. Carr surrendered to the inevitable, upon Uncle Beverly's death, and "turned, with the wasted energy of the unfit and the incompetent, to solve the inexplicable problem of indigent ladyhood."[27] Mrs. Peachey, however, sacrifices none of her beauty, charm, or serenity in running a boarding house:

> The room was the epitome of tragedy; yet in the centre of it, on one of the battered and broken-legged Heppelwhite chairs, sat Mrs. Peachey, rosy, plump, and pretty, regarding him with her quizzical smile. "Yes, life, of course, is sad if you stop to think about it," her smile seemed to assure him: "but the main thing, after all, is to be happy in spite of it."[28]

"Bleak, withered, austere,"[29] Mrs. Burden carries her cross as deserted wife, and grimly hangs on to life by means of the meager returns from her boardinghouse.

To Mrs. Upchurch, the admission of roomers into her home is no less distasteful, but Mrs. Upchurch is an opportunist, and has proved through the vicissitudes of a lifetime that she can cope with ups and downs. She has, moreover, a marriageable daughter, and it is safe to surmise that she will assist circumstances to produce for Annabel a wealthy husband. She is more astute to take advantage of opportunity in this field than Mrs. Carr or Mrs. Burden, similarly blessed with progeny.

The third "career" permitted gentlewomen dealt with sewing. Gabriella can sew all day, and yet move in the best society in the evening, but Gabriella has attractions, if not beauty. More usual in this occupation are Miss Polly Hatch and Miss Willy Whitlow. Miss Polly follows her trade unquestioningly, "a small indomitable spinster who sewed out by the day . . ." but by native endowment Miss Polly had no reason to expect or hope for a life pampered by male admiration.[30]

Miss Willy, responsible for most of the gowns in Dinwiddie and dispenser of a good part of its gossip, leans heavily upon her religion for moral support, for, in the words of Miss Batte:

> "How on earth could she go out sewing by the day if she didn't have her religious convictions?"[31]

Apparently religion supplies the only light in an otherwise barren, drab existence.

Rare instances occur, where ladies take to writing for a living. In *Virginia*, for example, the talkative Miss Batte recalls:

> "Why, when little Miss Amanda Sheppard was left at sixty without a roof over her head, she began at once, without saying a word to anybody, to write historical novels."[32]

Miss Batte feels obliged to stress, of course, Miss Amanda's financial need and the historical quality of the novels.

Veering away from the three "professions" tolerated for ladies, the novels of Ellen Glasgow introduce careers of modern scope. Gabriella overrules the objections of her family to engage in work outside the home, in a department store, where she learns the art of millinery. After the failure of her marriage to George Fowler, later on, she resumes this kind of work in earnest, and meets with great success in New York. She is a careerist in the modern sense of the word.

Gabriella exemplifies the most daring in her break with the past. By blood she is linked to the leisured class, but from her blood she gets the driving energy to express the spirit of revolt, to assert her independence in a new field, and there to make a notable success with her talents. Gabriella does not wholly escape her inheritance, which fosters conservatism and looks askance at the profession of actress:

> Not Mrs. Carr herself, not Cousin Becky Bollingbroke, of sanctified memory, could have regarded an actress's career with greater horror than did the advanced and independent Gabriella.[33]

If by some chance Gabriella had encountered Rachel Gavin in a New York street, or in an art gallery, it is highly probable that she would have experienced an instinctive repulsion from a woman who had combined a native talent for art with a conspicuous flair for the Bohemian life.[34]

The Builders, set in the years of the Great War, introduces a heroine in the modern role of nurse, Caroline Meade, whose family, though poor, is "good." Caroline's choice of a profession suits the period, and is appropriate to her character; it does not evolve solely from disappointment in love. The break in the betrothal may have given added impetus to the resolution gradually forming to help support her family by means of a congenial occupation that will allow full scope to her ambition and energy.

Dorinda Oakley approaches farming in the modern, scientific spirit, and reclaims, in *Barren Ground,* her father's farm through application of modern methods, which she studied in anticipation of the opportunity. In this novel Miss Glasgow travels to a different locale, to the Upper Valley of Virginia, in order to describe a woman successfully performing work usually considered exclusively man's domain. Dorinda descends from rugged, Scotch-Irish stock long familiar with farming, and is not restrained from activity by the restrictions imposed on women in the aristocratic region of the Tidewater. The career in agriculture possesses her utterly, and compensates, partially, for her disillusionment in love. In the last two novels of Miss Glasgow, heroines follow careers less from professional ambition than from an obligation to increase their husbands' incomes. Ada Fincastle McBride, in *Vein of Iron,* has also inherited indomitable courage from Scotch-Irish ancestry, which enables her to work hard hours in a department store in order to support her family during the trying years of the Depression. Roy Timberlake pretends enthusiasm for her work in an interior decorator's shop in *In This Our Life,* but chiefly because its financial returns allow her and Peter to get married. The latter novel reflects most decisively the changes in woman's social situation, from the Victorian ideal of woman as wife and mother, sheltered and supported by her husband, to the modern version of woman as wife and wage-earner, adding to her husband's income, but not raising a family. Woman has finally earned her freedom of choice, whether or not she makes good use of it, and has branched out from the three occupations which formerly limited opportunities for careers.

The arbitrary classifications—homemaker, frustrated spinster, gay lady, widow, and careerist—thus far used in describing the social category of Ellen Glasgow's heroines from antebellum days to the late 1930s, neglect an independent type of unmarried female whose emancipation may be traced from the womanly Amanda Lightfoot[35] to the versatile Corinna Page, a type that escapes, to some degree, male supremacy or financial worries.

Amanda Lightfoot faithfully observes Victorian modes of dress and thought. Wearing her hair pompadour-style still, in aloof disdain of new fashions, Amanda preserves intact her mental equilibrium, a sort of Victorian complacency, that admits no recognition of change, no movement of the wheels of progress. To her old families of Queensborough point with pride, a landmark fast growing into a legend because of her inviolate history. The respect with which she is regarded arises not so much from her unwavering loyalty to an idealized love as from her perfect demeanor, which lets fall no hint of disappointment, no reproach toward a lover who has not reciprocated her loyalty. Cast in a particular mold from birth, she has no capacity to change with the times, is less likely to give vent to any spontaneous expression of thought or feeling than Edmonia Bredalbane is apt to observe the formalities of conduct which appeal so strongly to her twin brother, the Judge, in theory.

In contrast to the slightly sad, although sweetly smiling, Amanda—wrapped in the gossamer of her fifty-eight years of maidenhood—are the refreshing glimpses of Louise Goddard, in *They Stooped to Folly*, and Corinna Page, in *One Man in His Time*. Louisa, who stands midway between Amanda and Corinna, "had travelled far since the artificial eighties, when spinsters, like husbands, had preferred sweetness to light."[36] Louisa, considered by Judge Littlepage unusually good-looking for a reformer, is "the only thorn in his comforting theory that bachelors make themselves while Providence makes spinsters."[37] "Even from the chivalrous angle, it was impossible to think of her as discarded by life."[38] She disguises a deep affection for Mr. Littlepage under a facial expression of good humor and tolerance. Even if her best friend, Victoria, is married to the man she has always loved, Louisa carries her disappointment with philosophic calm, and directs her energies into intellectual

and charitable channels. Her life does not end with the failure
of romance.

Corinna Page gets the most value out of her leisure and
money, opening her print shop with the explanation, "A shop
is the only place where you may have calls from people who
haven't been introduced to you.[39] In Stephen Culpeper's admiring
eyes:

> At forty-eight she was lovelier, he thought, than ever; she would
> always be lovelier than any one else if she lived to be ninety.
> There wasn't a girl in his set who could compare with her,
> wasn't one who had the singing heart of Corinna.[40]

Her heart insists on singing, while her eyes see things as they are:

> In Corinna . . . two opposing spirits had battled unceasingly,
> the realistic spirit which accepted life as it was, and the romantic
> spirit which struggled toward some unattainable perfection, which
> endeavored to change and decorate the actuality. More than
> Stephen, perhaps, she had faced life; but she had not accepted
> it without rebellion. She had learned from disappointment to see
> things as they are; but deep in her heart some unspent fire of
> romance, some imprisoned aesthetic impulse, sought continually
> to enrich the experience of the moment.[41]

Corinna leads a life far from narrow, in her relationship to
other people, in her grasp of essential verities, in her intellectual
freedom, and in her emotional maturity. With Gideon Vetch,
the people's governor, she is proud to be friends, having weighed
his sense of humanity against his lack of education and appre-
ciating his worth.

Corinna and Gabriella depart from customary behavior ap-
proved by the inner circle of Virginians, and assess wisely the
qualities, if not the quality, of men in their lives. Gabriella, at
length, flees from the arms of the patient Southern gentleman
into the arms of his exact opposite, Ben O'Hara, whose genuine
goodness and strength of character outweigh his cultural defects.

Life and Gabriella (1916) antedates World War I. *One Man
in His Time* (1922) closely follows it. They forecast modern

woman, and emphasize her postwar vitality in an era and a place where the old type of womanly woman still figured. They show that even against strong opposition from a section of the country that has always been regimented against change, contradictions were appearing during these momentous decades. Establishing the fact that genteel ladies prevailed even into the twenties, they prove the coexistence of rebels in the postwar decade who were surely creating a different concept of women. They show, in this transitional period, customs that have departed from usage and customs that linger on longer only to die from exposure to the robust spirit of the twenties.

A consideration of women's situation in Virginia should take some cognizance of the status of black women. The subject offers too many ramifications in reference to the race problem, sufficiently important to warrant a separate study, to allow more than brief suggestions here on the author's treatment. Ellen Glasgow takes her place among those who have truly caught the spirit of the Southern black, in rendition of dialect, temperament, character, and customs.

We should not be too greatly surprised at her unhesitating use of situations in miscegenation, done honestly and fairly when the plot so requires. Her domineering "mammies" and beautiful mulattoes become involved in such affairs as George Birdsong's with the laundress Memoria. Cyrus Treadwell feels no responsibility for Jubal, his son by the washwoman Mandy, and, in later years, when she humbly asks for help, he explodes:

> "It's a pretty pass things have come to when men have to protect themselves from Negro women."[42]

The same evening, after refusing assistance for Jubal, he starts to make a call on young Oliver Treadwell, his nephew, reflecting:

> "Even if the boy's a fool, I'm not one to let those of my own blood come to want."[43]

The irony of his attitude repeats itself in Mr. Littlepage's meticulous remembrance of the past:

When they wished to misconduct themselves, they had, with such notorious exceptions as Colonel Bletheram, stepped down discreetly from their superior station in life; and in the ages of gallantry, which were undaunted by the perils of miscegenation, they had stepped down also from their superior shading in colour. These unpleasant truths, thought Mr. Littlepage, who had become resigned to the universe, are the facts of life that every man discovers, and no man discusses.[44]

He faces a fine point of honor, in a discussion with his wife:

"I am merely reminding you that the seduction of a woman does constitute some sort of moral claim on a decent man. When there has been a child, the claim would appear to become stronger."

Mrs. Littlepage interpolates an embarrassing question:

"Why, I thought you argued just the other way a few days ago about your Uncle Mark . . ."

He explains, "with legal punctilio":

"But that . . . was the case of a mulatto child."[45]

These extracts, brief as they are, illustrate the author's comprehending, but uncompromising, exposition of the drama furnished by women of the Negro race down South. Minerva and Memoria are noble women, reduced to servility by reason of their color.[46]

ECONOMICAL SITUATION

The social situation of women in the Southland, so definitely confined and so clearly defined in the novels of Ellen Glasgow, found no latitude for development in economic, religious, intellectual, or political fields. Woman entertained no ambition in these matters held to be, almost constitutionally, men's domain. Her social situation dictated autocratically the narrow boundaries of self-expression, which, naturally, did not extend to interests so manifestly unsuitable. She existed in a vacuum, protected from contamination by economic, political, religious, and educational thought.

Economically the women in Ellen Glasgow's novels appear in two groupings. The typical, Southern gentlewoman, whether solicitous wife, widowed or spinster relative, or tarnished lady depends completely upon the gallantry of men for support. The "new" woman, whether offspring of the "good families" or of the "good people," has the initiative and temerity to break away from traditional attitudes and restraints, seeking within herself the means and strength of self-support. Examples of the first, being more typical, are more prevalent in the comedies of manners.

Bred in almost every Southern lady was the resolution to find a husband who would take care of her for the rest of her idyllic life. When poverty obliges Angelica Blackburn, in *The Builders*, to choose between teaching and marrying, she decides on the second alternative, even without love, as the lesser of two evils. The woman lacking a husband was a woman socially and economically handicapped. By her contemporaries she was viewed as a failure—condescendingly, if she had not the necessary charm to attract a proposal, like Aunt Kesiah; sympathetically, if she had been disappointed in love, like martyred Amanda Lightfoot; suspiciously, if she continued to prey on the susceptibilities of married, but still gallant, gentlemen; and coldly, if she had ever forgotten herself, like poor Aunt Agatha. The successful performance of woman revolved around her relationship to man. At no other time or place has there flourished a society where women leaned more heavily upon men, who, to justify their illusions of the feminine ideal, unprotestingly and dutifully bore the costly brunt of their support. Mrs. Blake, in *The Deliverance*, voices the general opinion, in recommending marriage to her son:

> He has remained single too long as it is, for, as dear old Bishop Deane used to say, it is surely the duty of every gentleman to take upon himself the provision of at least one helpless female.

. . . "I never blamed your poor father one instant—not even
for the loss of my six children, which certainly would not have
happened if I had not married him. But, as I've often told you,
my dear, I think marriage should be rightly regarded more as a
duty than as a pleasure. Your Aunt Susannah always said it was
like choosing a partner at a ball; for my part, I think it resembles
more the selecting of a brand of flour."[47]

Disapprobation of spinsters is one of her strong prejudices,
modulated not a particle by the fact that the Blake family
contains two unmarried daughters, one of whom, Cynthia, is an
inevitable and unfortunate example:

"As for Cynthia, she is out of the question, of course, which
is a great pity. I have very little patience with an unmarried
woman—no, not if she were Queen Elizabeth herself—though I
do know that they are sometimes found very useful in the dairy
or the spinning-room."[48]

To her younger daughter, Lila, she returns to the refrain:

"I have always urged it as a duty, not advised it as a
pleasure. As far as that goes, I hold to this day the highest
opinion of matrimony and men, though I admit, when I con-
sider the attention they require, I sometimes feel that women
might select a better object."[49]

Mrs. Blake has long ago given up hope for the plain, middle-
aged Cynthia. Unprepossessing as Aunt Kesiah in *The Miller of
Old Church*, Cynthia lacks any ambition except that of preserving appearances, at all costs. Contriving to keep her blind
mother in ignorance of their fallen fortunes, of Christopher's
manual labor and her own drudgery, she cultivates another illusion—that the younger sister, Lila, must be shielded from all
demeaning toil and must be prepared to make an aristocratic,
wealthy marriage. She spins out her daydreams on these shaky
assumptions, clinging for reassurance to past glories of the family.
Christopher, depressed with bitterness over his lost inheritance,
seconds her pretenses, and gives almost his life's blood to eke
out a living for his three, dependent women folks.

Poverty, inertia, and ill health served as direct causes in forcing gentlewomen into the economic category of dependent relatives. Controlling these factors, however indirectly, was the social stigma attached to activities outside the home, except for teaching and sewing, which would have interfered with any considerable assertion against an unenviable condition, and must be considered.

There is the case of the two impoverished gentlewomen who board at Mrs. Carr's. Left destitute in their old age, they lead a precarious existence in contriving to live and to preserve their gentility:

> Two elderly spinsters, bearing the lordly, though fallen, name of Peterborough . . . spent their lives in a beautiful and futile pretense—the pretense of keeping up an appearance. They also took in the plain sewing of their richer relatives, who lived in Franklin Street, and sent them little trays of sweet things as soon as the midday dinner was over on Sunday. Sometimes they would drop in to see Mrs. Carr just before supper was ready, and then they would pretend that they lived on tea and toast because they were naturally "light eaters," and that they sewed all day, not for the money, but because they liked to have "something to do with their hands." They were tall thin women in organdie caps and black alpaca dresses made with long basques which showed a greenish cast in the daylight.[50]

Gabriella Carr, newly wedded to George Fowler and expected to move in New York society, has no allowance, but must endure the humiliation of asking her husband for every little sum, from carfare to the price of a new gown. Her mother, Mrs. Carr, has always operated on the theory that the nearest male relative will come to the rescue in any financial dilemma:

> So deeply rooted in her being was the instinct to twine, that for the first few years of her bereavement she had simply sat in her widow's weeds, with her rent paid by Cousin Jimmy Wrenn and her market bills settled monthly by Uncle Beverly Blair, and waited patiently for some man to come and support her.[51]

Her daughter is differently constituted, however, and pressed for money, cheerfully and firmly discards checks on a career, dives headlong into the fashion mart of New York, and builds up a reputation as a highly successful milliner. She sloughs simultaneously the bonds of an unsatisfactory marriage and of prejudice, risking disapproval for not making the best of a bad bargain with George and inviting censure by entering the business world.

In this day and age, which safeguards, by law, rights of women over their property and over custodianship of their children, it is possible to forget that the preceding century did not assure such rights, until years had passed, and then only tentative gestures were made in certain states.[52] Man controlled the pursestrings and doled out spending money to his wife according to the dictates of his nature. Like Gabriella, Mrs. Cyrus Treadwell has little or no money from her husband. The stark tragedy of her long endurance comes out when she urges upon her penniless nephew the sum of fifty dollars:

> "I've saved this up for six months. . . . It came from selling some silver forks that belonged to the Bolingbrokes, and I've always felt easier to think that I had a little laid away that he had nothing to do with. From the very day that I married him, he was always close about money."[53]

This from the wife of the richest man in Dinwiddie! Farther on she adds:

> "I can help you a little more after a while. . . . I'm raising a few squabs out in the back yard, and Meadows is going to buy them as soon as they are big enough to eat."[54]

General Archibald supports a large household of dependent relatives in *The Sheltered Life*, including his only son's widow and child, two unmarried daughters, and "the usual number of indigent cousins and aunts."[55] His daughter-in-law, Cora, has resigned herself to the passive state of widowhood:

> Still disposed to fill out in the wrong places, she had pulled in the strings of her stays and settled down into security. After all, one could bear any discomfort of body so long as one was not obliged to be independent in act.[56]

Corinna, the widowed Mrs. Kent Page, does not belong to the usual type of luckless females reduced to widowhood, for, at forty-eight, she still has wealth, beauty, charm, and in defiance of custom, she circulates freely in society to enjoy life far from static or empty. But Corinna is the rare exception to the rule, who finds her way into one of Miss Glasgow's novels[57] by deliberate intention of the author to show, by contrast, what could be done, granted an individuality, toward broadening and intensifying the capacity of woman to live; even a woman whose matrimonial state no longer secured the base of her pedestal. Corinna represents the democratic ideal in her generous sympathies, directness, honesty, fairness, intellect, and culture. She shows what a resourceful woman can become.

Uncertain sources of income harass the gay, sophisticated ladies, like Mrs. Dalrymple, who keep very busy cultivating favor with masculine benefactors. Amy, being a practical soul, maneuvers, with extreme delicacy and adroitness to achieve her ends. She gives an inkling of her method in her musings:

> "If you're careful, card sense will stay by you when you need it, and sometimes put money in your pocket long after you have lost your looks. But presents, even if they are set in platinum, go out of fashion." Then, since she had been a realist from the beginning, before the bottom dropped out of idealism, she determined to be guided by prudence rather than generosity in every love affair that came after fifty.[58]

Her revery, in meeting up with a potential lover in Mr. Littlepage, sums up her situation:

> Though she nourished few illusions, and none of these dealt with the nature of man, she had not failed to observe that for a Southern lady in reduced circumstances and with an impaired reputation, love is the only available means of increasing an income.[59]

Of course Judge Honeywell is justified in extending a helping hand to flighty Annabel, for kinship makes the gesture quite proper:

> It was true that he had intended to look after Cordelia's poor
> relations; and of them all, numerous as they were, there was no
> doubt in his mind that Annabel was her favorite. . . . Encour-
> aged by the sense of duty, he continued almost gaily: "You must
> have that dress, Annabel. I'll send a cheque to your mother the
> first thing in the morning."[60]

Leaving Annabel, Mrs. Carr, and Mrs. Dalrymple to the
tender mercies of their nearest male connections, we turn from
the comedies of manners to the epic novels of Miss Glasgow
for a view of heroines wringing a successful living from a hostile
world. The most triumphant character in Miss Glasgow's row
of illuminated portraits finds her salvation in *Barren Ground.*
The intensified atmosphere of unrelieved toil, hardship, and
poverty—Russian in its somberness—makes Dorinda Oakley's victory more pronounced. She sheds the illusion of romantic youth,
with her infatuation for Jason Greylock; she absorbs herself in
developing her farm scientifically and profitably. While Jason's
farm deteriorates, hers produces. She sets a strenuous pace for
competing, neighboring farmers, becoming, at the same
time, a smart and keen business woman who finds a meaning
for living in the satisfaction of work. Just as she saves her land
from the broomsedge, she rescues her own life from the weeds
of doubt, distrust, bitterness, and despair, which had almost
ruined it, and reaps, at last, the rewards of courage, faith, and
hope.

Dorinda conquers her fate by her self-reliance, and owes to
no man her rise in prosperity. She is modern in every feature,
looking forward, not backward, applying immense quantities of
thought and energy to her undertakings, and exhibiting, throughout, an indestructible self-sufficiency. Her victory is complete,
for she arrives at middle-age not at all embittered by her ordeal,
but capable of reaching out a strong hand to help her defeated
deceiver, Jason Greylock.

Ada Fincastle never acquires Dorinda's wealth, but, in *Vein
of Iron,* she lives from day to day, the moral prop of an irresolute
husband and the principal means of support for her husband,
son, and father. She has only her meager pay envelope from

the department store with which to face the economic problems
of the thirties. Although Ada lacks the drive and shrewdness,
which were responsible for Dorinda's financial success, she shares
with the heroine of *Barren Ground* qualities of character and
indefatigable strength that can contest economic handicaps and
never admit defeat.

It is somewhat of a relief to become acquainted with heroines
like Ada and Dorinda when the progression of Southern ladies
has yielded so much proof of the economic supremacy of man,
if we except the anachronisms of Gabriella Carr and Corinna
Page.[61] The pathos of the old order, of feminine obscurity and
feminine defeatism, wherein women "waited on" the stinginess
or largesse of men, gives ground gradually to the security of a
new balance of power, signalizing the advent of a new breed
of women into affairs of the world—women adequately constituted to earn and preserve their economic independence.

POLITICAL SITUATION

History tells us that movements for the abolition of slavery,
for temperance, and for women's suffrage, which furnished the
most controversial, picturesque activity for the latter half of the
nineteenth and early part of the twentieth centuries, occurred
almost simultaneously, promoted by the same crusading individuals and groups.[62]

The innocuous, helpless position of woman, as first conceived
in novels by Ellen Glasgow, may be partly attributed to the
institution of slavery. As one sociologist has pointed out, a privileged class which tolerated and profited from slavery of a race
was not inclined to feel compunction or concern over the strait-
ened lives of women.[63] Miss Nell Battle Lewis, in the *Raleigh
News and Observer*,[64] reported that slavery

> Acted to dull the South's conception of individual liberty as the
> greatest boon of all mankind and made the lack of such liberty
> in the case of women seem less important and less deplorable
> than it otherwise might have appeared.

Frozen attitudes and hardened conventions supported the fallacy of woman's inferiority, and persisted in restricting women's rights, socially, economically, politically, and educationally.

Politically speaking, the times and places of Ellen Glasgow's novels offer no opportunity for the exploits of her heroines. History reminds us that the persevering efforts to secure women the right to vote did not produce tangible results until the Nineteenth Amendment was passed in 1919. Furthermore, ratification by three-fourths of the states consumed another year, and did not number Virginia, the Carolinas, Georgia, Florida, Mississippi, and Louisiana among its supporters. The atmosphere was not at all conducive to feminine participation in politics, especially in the South, where reaction was firmly intrenched. Up to 1920, except for a certain amount of agitation in the North, women had few, if any, political rights.

Whatever influence the heroines of Ellen Glasgow exercised over their masculine friends, so far as politics is concerned, does not survive for the record. Instances of concern with politics are indirect and negligible. In *The Voice of the People*, Eugenia Battle appears almost a passive spectator to her husband's career, except as she furthers his prestige through her gracious hospitality to his political acquaintances. Corinna Page, in *One Man in His Time*, evinces considerable interest in political ideas, but serves more as an attentive audience to Governor Vetch than as an adviser. The day of woman's admission into politics did not claim Miss Glasgow's immediate attention. Woman's social status, with its adjuncts of economic and intellectual situations, occupied her almost exclusively.

RELIGIOUS SITUATION

The religious propensities of the characters in Ellen Glasgow's comedies rarely stray from the inherited beliefs and observances of the Protestant Episcopal Church:

> Religion, which made so much trouble in New England, had softened in a milder climate, among an Episcopal society at

least, to a healthful moral exercise and a comfortable sense of Divine favour.[65]

Adherence to the prescribed faith belonged among a gentleman's or a lady's primary obligations, however shallow-rooted. Although Miss Glasgow respects the rector in *Virginia*, that high-minded, idealistic, impractical individual, she displays frequent amusement over many of his parishioners.

Cyrus Treadwell, whose weekday methods of amassing money would scarcely pass inspection in a Higher Court, occupies his pew faithfully on Sunday, and, as his attacks of dyspepsia multiply, increases the size and number of his checks to the Church. Miss Priscilla Batte proposes a logical solution for resolving Oliver Treadwell's upset mental condition and intellectual revolt:

> "What he needed was merely some good girl to take care of him and convert him to the Episcopal Church."[66]

In her eyes the Church can be relied upon to furnish the panacea for nearly any mental disturbance.

On the other hand, Mrs. Littlepage is less certain of the efficacy of this remedy, for her new son-in-law, Martin Welding, and cautions her strenuous daughter, Mary Victoria, against forcing him to attend church with her. Mary Victoria argues that her father had always attended St. Luke's with her mother, but her mother patiently points out that Martin should not be judged by Mr. Littlepage. Mary Victoria invariably has the last word:

> "We've always been religious, mother, and nice people in Queensborough go to church no matter what they believe."[67]

The confidence felt by "nice people in Queensborough" for the Church is reflected elsewhere; in Mr. Littlepage's thoughts, for instance:

> All the learning required to make a Southern gentleman was comprised, as every Littlepage knew without being told, in the

calf-bound rows of classic authors and the Prayer-Book of the Protestant Episcopal Church.[68]

The association of ideas links the Church with some other Southern forms, in the mind of Mrs. Dalrymple:

> Never, until she engaged in active combat, had she been able to understand how the sex that invented battle and murder and rape could have invented also, without a change of heart apparently, monogamy and the perfect lady and the Protestant Episcopal Church.[69]

Of General Archibald, the philosopher, the man of honor, Miss Glasgow comments:

> Though the poet in him was lost, he became in later years a prosperous attorney, and a member in good standing, so long as one did not inquire too closely, of the Episcopal Church.[70]

His daughter-in-law, Cora, regards anyone outside their Church with suspicion, and makes it difficult for Joseph Crocker, handicapped by overalls and adherence to the Baptist Church, to woo Isabella Archibald.

Margaret Blair, a womanly young woman from *One Man in His Time*, who has been brought up most correctly and will, one day, the families devoutly hope, grace Stephen Culpeper's hearth and who typifies the woman restrained, willingly enough, from branching out from the sheltered perimeter of a lady's existence, tells us in a conversation with Stephen how little her religion means or brings to her:

> "But you are a man. . . . Everything is easier for a man. You can go out and do things."
> "So can women now. You can even go into politics."
> "Oh, I've been too well brought up! There isn't any hope for a girl who is well brought up except the church, and even there she can't do anything but sit and listen to sermons.[71]

From these quotations only one conclusion may be derived: that the Protestant Episcopal Church comprised part of a gentlewoman's inheritance, in Virginia, and was faithfully, if not enthusiastically, supported. Church attendance was observed punctiliously, and the forms of worship were repeated without the consciousness of their original significance. Religion had declined to outward observance without spiritual meaning.

Barren Ground and *Vein of Iron* show manifestations of religion in more violent convictions. Among the Scotch-Irish descendants of the inland, farming country, stern religiosity provides the main, emotional outlet, and, in the former novel, may be held responsible for urging Mrs. Oakley close to the brink of insanity. At the end of the long, hard workday on the farm, she gathers her family together in her room and reads the most forboding passages of the Bible to them, the lines emphasizing the waiting wrath of Almighty God against sinners on earth. Although religion motivates her life, it does not fortify her against committing perjury to save her son from punishment for murder. What these followers of Presbyterianism extract from their religion is not an understanding of the tenderness implicit in the teachings of Christ, not trust in the forms and ceremonies that beautify some doctrines, but a sense of the omnipresence of an all-powerful, judging Deity.

Grandma Fincastle, in *Vein of Iron*, is a stout Presbyterian believer, bitterly irreconcilable to sin, and when Ada's fall from grace becomes apparent, she refuses to have anything to do with her granddaughter, or to speak to her. Only at the moment of painful childbirth does she capitulate, discard her principles, and share her courage with Ada for the ordeal.

Sarah Revercomb, in *The Miller of Old Church*, ferociously stands by her Baptist religion, against the persuasions of the family, who have joined the rest of the community in going over to the Episcopal faith, appealingly represented by a new young rector, the handsome Orlando Mullen.

The prominent religions in Ellen Glasgow's novels are the Protestant Episcopal and the Presbyterian. Her heroines, whether in the comedies of manners or in the epic tales, do not appear too deeply affected. In the former, they observe the religious amenities as part of their cultural obligations. In the latter, they conform without succumbing seriously to the dreary philosophy.

EDUCATIONAL SITUATION

The possession of intellect can be regarded as a doubtful blessing for women of the South in the nineteenth century, who, among the genteel classes, cultivated the supreme ambition of epitomizing man's ideals, if not of satisfying his desires. Susan Treadwell, daughter of the richest man in Dinwiddie, finds her chances of further education stunted at the roots, although to her cousin Oliver she has confessed:

> "I've thought sometimes that I should almost be willing to starve if only I might go to college."[72]

Her father's reaction to her extraordinary request could have been anticipated, and is certainly designed to dissipate her foolish notions:

> "Tut-tut. . . . If you want something to occupy you, you'd better start helping your mother with her preserving."[73]

When Susan asks him to lend her the money, promising to pay it back as soon as she gets a position, he reminds her that she can repay him for her schooling at Miss Batte's.

Then follows, in the author's best manner, a definition of education in Dinwiddie, feminine style:

> Few, indeed, were the girls born in Dinwiddie since the war who had not learned reading, penmanship ("up to the right, down to the left, my dear"), geography, history, arithmetic, deportment, and the fine arts, in the Academy for Young Ladies. The brilliant record of the General still shed a legendary lustre upon the school, and it was earnestly believed that no girl, after leaving there with a diploma for good conduct, could possibly go wrong or become eccentric in her later years. To be sure, she might remain a trifle weak in her spelling (Miss Priscilla having, as he

confessed, a poor head for that branch of study), but, after all, as the rector had once remarked, good spelling is by no means a necessary accomplishment for a lady; and it was certain that the moral education of a pupil of the academy would be firmly rooted in such fundamental verities as the superiority of man and the aristocratic supremacy of the Episcopal Church.[74]

The most that a girl of Susan's intelligence could hope for, before the days of woman's emancipation, was the prevailing, prescribed tutelage of a Miss Batte, which equipped her for living up to the finest traditions of Southern womanhood but omitted the faintest inkling of the means for facing life.

The Reverend Orlando Mullen voices the attitude, in a sermon to his flock at Old Church:

> "Woman . . . was created to look after the ways of her household in order that man might go out into the world and make a career. No womanly woman cared to make a career. What the womanly woman desired was to remain an Incentive, an Ideal, an Inspiration."[75]

Uncle Meriwether exhibits Cyrus Treadwell's antipathy to feminine education, "this new-fangled nonsense,"[76] which would not help women to be any better mothers and wives, but might, conceivably so demoralize them as to incite them to run away from their husbands.

Miss Glasgow's first novel, *The Descendant*, which uses New York for a setting, introduces Mrs. Semple who has been working actively for the emancipation of women. The hero, Michael Akershem, an expatriated Virginian, observes with amazement the deference in Mr. Semple's manner to her:

> There was no turn in the conversation that he did not appeal to her judgment; when she spoke he listened gravely; if he differed he entered into a full argument.[77]

During the years of the First World War the advanced David Blackburn comes to a sudden realization in conversation with Caroline Meade:

It had never occurred to him that a woman could become companionable on intellectual grounds.[78]

The financier, Mr. Fowler, who has moved his family from Virginia to New York City, treats his wife as if she were a dream woman:

> From the first minute it was evident to Gabriella that her father-in-law adored his wife as an ideal, though he seemed scarcely aware of her as a person. He had given her his love, but his interests, his energies, his attention were elsewhere.[79]

Woman's intellectual entity did not materialize fully until the 1920s, but clung, in the Old Dominion, to the ideal incarnated in Virginia, whom Miss Batte called

> a "docile" pupil, meaning one who deferentially submitted her opinions to her superiors, and to go through life perpetually submitting her opinions was, in the eyes of her parents and her teacher, the divinely appointed task of woman. Her education was founded upon the simple theory that the less a girl knew about life, the better prepared she could be to contend with it. Knowledge of any sort (except the rudiments of reading and writing, the geography of countries she would never visit, and the dates of battles in ancient history) was kept from her as rigorously as if it contained the germs of a contagious disease.[80]

The educational outlook of Ellen Glasgow's heroines in the comedies of manners is bleak, streotyped, and provincial. Miss Glasgow left a lasting record of a civilization that pampered its women and repressed them, that resented and dismissed any fleeting impulses toward learning, that yielded tardily and begrudgingly to intellectual independence in the new century. The author's method is admirable, free of invective or tirade, deftly ironical and witty, and humanely compassionate. Her criticism proves the waste and cruelty of a system that leaves the beautiful Virginias helplessly vulnerable to life and that frustrates the ambitious Susans in intellectual aspirations.

NOTES

1. *The Battle-Ground*, 48.
2. *The Miller of Old Church*, 70.
3. *Ibid.*, 74.
4. *Ibid.*, 75.
5. *Ibid.*, 72.
6. *Ibid.*, 79.
7. *Life and Gabriella*, 311.
8. *The Sheltered Life, The Miller of Old Church, The Battle-Ground, The Romance of a Plain Man.*
9. *The Romance of a Plain Man*, 212.
10. *Ibid.*, 206.
11. *Ibid.*, 398.
12. *They Stooped to Folly*, 85.
13. *Ibid.*, 85.
14. *Ibid.*, 26.
15. *Ibid.*, 350.
16. *Ibid.*, 138.
17. *Ibid.*, 293.
18. *Ibid.*, 331.
19. *The Romantic Comedians*, 17.
20. *Ibid.*, 77-78.
21. *A Certain Measure*, 83.
22. *Life and Gabriella*, 8.
23. *Ibid.*, 17.
24. *The Romantic Comedians*, 118.
25. *Virginia*, 10.
26. *Life and Gabriella*, 26.
27. *Ibid.*, 9.
28. *Virginia*, 110-11.
29. *They Stooped to Folly*, 225.
30. *Life and Gabriella*, 77.
31. *Virginia*, 17.
32. *Ibid.*, 19.
33. *Life and Gabriella*, 375-76.
34. *The Descendant.*
35. *The Romantic Comedians.*
36. *They Stooped to Folly*, 257.
37. *Ibid.*, 275.
38. *Ibid.*
39. *One Man in His Time*, 37.
40. *Ibid.*, 37-38.

41. *Ibid.*, 341.
42. *Virginia*, 157.
43. *Ibid.*, 158.
44. *They Stooped to Folly*, 69.
45. *Ibid.*, 258-59.
46. *In This Our Life; The Sheltered Life.*
47. *The Deliverance*, 200-201.
48. *Ibid.*, 159.
49. *Ibid.*, 399.
50. *Life and Gabriella*, 13.
51. *Ibid.*, 8.
52. Mississippi, in 1839, was the first state to grant control over their own property to married women.
53. *Virginia*, 102.
54. *Ibid.*, 103-4.
55. *The Sheltered Life*, 24.
56. *Ibid.*
57. *One Man in His Time.*
58. *They Stooped to Folly*, 102.
59. *Ibid.*, 101.
60. *Ibid.*, 22-23.
61. *Life and Gabriella; One Man in His Time.*
62. Virginius Dabney, *Liberalism in the South* (Chapel Hill, University of North Carolina Press, 1932), 30.
63. *Ibid.*, 363.
64. *Raleigh News and Observer*, April 19, 26; May 3, 10, 17, 24, 1925.
65. *A Certain Measure*, 136.
66. *Virginia*, 125.
67. *They Stooped to Folly*, 191.
68. *Ibid.*, 77
69. *Ibid.*, 101.
70. *The Sheltered Life*, 163.
71. *One Man in His Time*, 85.
72. *Virginia*, 96.
73. *Ibid.*, 148.
74. *Ibid.*, 10-11.
75. *The Miller of Old Church*, 130.
76. *Life and Gabriella*, 22.
77. *The Descendant*, 164.
78. *The Builders*, 234.
79. *Life and Gabriella*, 128.
80. *Virginia*, 20.

VI
Conclusion

Intending a social history of the Commonwealth, Ellen Glasgow developed her canvas broadly to represent fully and accurately the status quo, the transition, and the readjustments in the scene from antebellum days through 1939. She saw the privileged class in the throes of change, giving way gradually to the will of the people. She projected this social upheaval with all its reverberating consequences to men and to values, and expressed confidence that it would infuse new hope and health into a decadent culture.

The part woman plays is not at all diminutive against this impressive background. It furnishes many of the highlights of the tapestry, tracing the social, economical, and educational patterns, and allowing inspection from many angles. The technique of the artist is subtle, and yet it is definite. Her meaning is quite clear in the individual portraits.

Virginia cannot be derided as inanimate. She has sufficient will and mentality, but directs them, under pressure of custom and training, into the wrong channels. Gabriella's self-assertiveness points up the sacrifice of Virginia's personality. Each woman character illustrates by her example, good or bad, the need to develop her own individuality, to strengthen her intestinal fortitude and her capacity to live. The flesh and blood must live like flesh and blood. Dorinda Oakley and Ada Fincastle know this lesson, and Gabriella discovers it.

Whether Ellen Glasgow's treatment adopted an ironic vein in the comedies of manners, or used a serious tone in the epic novels, it depicted with truth and reality situations of women that are universally typical. The aristocratic society of the Tidewater and the middle class of the Valley of Virginia provided a wide range of material between the years 1850 and 1939, enough to authenticate a specific history of woman—wife, mother, spinster, gay lady, and careerist—as she existed in Virginia.

In the Old Dominion, woman's social situation, based upon false ideals of chivalry, impoverished her for generations. Denied the right to expand, coerced by the gentle, but tyrannical, bonds of sentimentalism and evasive idealism, woman flowered, without flourishing, for almost a century. What Miss Glasgow did, through application of astute perception, consummate artistry, and unrelaxing good taste, was to tear to shreds the veil of illusion, to release woman from a constricting shelter, to secure recognition for her native endowment of brains, intellect, and ability, and to prepare the way for the expression of her personality and individuality.

In accomplishing so much for the Southern gentlewoman, Miss Glasgow stated the case for women everywhere, who have known a defeat in life through restricted opportunity. The fashions in life change, but the human relationships continue to depend upon basic adjustments among the living. The liberation of the human spirit is as real a necessity today as when Ellen Glasgow wrote. The lesson implicit in her treatment of the social situation of women may serve a timeless purpose, in fostering and preserving more generous and more understanding attitudes.

Selected Bibliography

WORKS OF ELLEN GLASGOW

Novels

The Ancient Law. New York: Doubleday, Page and Company, 1908.

Barren Ground. New York: Modern Library (Random House), 1933 (1925).

The Battle-Ground. New York: Doubleday, Page and Company, 1902.

The Builders. Garden City, New York: Doubleday, Page and Company, 1919.

The Deliverance. New York: Doubleday, Page and Company, 1904.

The Descendant. New York: Harper and Brothers Publishers, 1897.

In This Our Life. New York: Harcourt, Brace and Company, 1941.

Life and Gabriella. Garden City, New York: Doubleday, Page and Company, 1916.

The Miller of Old Church. Garden City, New York: Doubleday, Page and Company, 1911.

One Man in His Time. Garden City, New York: Doubleday, Page and Company, 1922.

Phases of an Inferior Planet. New York: Harper and Brothers Publishers, 1898.

The Romance of a Plain Man. New York: A. L. Burt Company, 1910 (1909).

74

The Romantic Comedians. Garden City, New York: Doubleday, Doran and Company, Country Life Press (The Old Dominion Edition), 1937 (1926).

The Sheltered Life. Garden City, New York: Doubleday, Doran and Company, Inc., 1932.

They Stooped to Folly. Garden City, New York: Doubleday, Doran and Company, Country Life Press (The Old Dominion Edition), 1929.

Vein of Iron. New York: Harcourt, Brace and Company, 1935.

Virginia. Garden City, New York: Doubleday, Doran and Company, Country Life Press (The Old Dominion Edition), 1929 (1913).

The Voice of the People. New York: Doubleday, Page and Company, 1900.

The Wheel of Life. New York: Doubleday, Page and Company, 1906.

Miscellaneous Works

A Certain Measure; an Interpretation of Prose Fiction. New York: Harcourt, Brace and Company, 1943 (1938).

"Feminism, a Definition." *Good Housekeeping,* LVIII (May 1914), 683.

"Heroes and Monsters" in *What Is a Book?* Dale Warren, ed. Boston: Houghton, Mifflin and Company, 1935, 15-20.

"Jordan's End; Story with Biographical Note." *Scholastic,* XL (January 22, 1945), 21-22.

"What I Believe." *The Nation,* CXXXVI (April 12, 1933), 404-6.

BIBLIOGRAPHIES

Edly, William H. "Bibliography of Ellen Anderson Gholson Glasgow." *Bulletin of Bibliography,* XVII (September-December 1940), 47-50.

"Bibliography." *A Certain Measure.* New York: Harcourt, Brace and Company, 1943, 265-72.

BIOGRAPHIES

Overton, Grant M. "Ellen Glasgow's Arrow." *Bookman,* LXI (May 1925), 291-96.
Publishers' Weekly, CXLVIII (December 1, 1945), 2448 (obituary).
Richardson, Eudora Ramsay. "Richmond and Its Writers." *Bookman,* LXVIII (December 1928), 449-53.
Time, XXXVII (March 31, 1941) ("Blood and Irony," review of *In This Our Life*), 72-74.
Tyler, Alice M. "Ellen Glasgow: Her Books and Her Personality," *Book News,* XXX (August 1912), 843-48.
Who's Who in America, 1946-47, XXIV 878-79.
Willett, Fred B. *Contemporary American Authors.* New York: Harcourt, Brace and Company, 1940, 374.
The Wilson Library Bulletin, IV (May 1930), 424. XX (January 1946), 328.

COMMENTARIES

Adams, James Donald. *The Shape of Books to Come.* New York: Viking Press, 1944, passim.
———. *Treasure Chest.* New York: E. P. Dutton, Publishers, 1946, 289-94.
Brickell, Herschel. "Miss Glasgow and Mr. Marquand." *Virginia Quarterly Review,* XVII (July 1941), 405-17.
Cabell, James Branch. *Let Me Lie.* New York: Farrar, Straus and Company, 1947, 80; 229-67.
———. *Some of Us.* New York: Robert M. McBride, 1930, 45-58.
———. "Two Sides of the Shielded." *New York Herald Tribune Books,* April 20, 1930, 11.
Canby, Henry Seidel. "Ellen Glasgow; Ironic Tragedian." *The Saturday Review of Literature,* XVIII (September 10, 1938), 3-14.
———. "Saturday Review of Literature Award to Ellen Glasgow." *The Saturday Review of Literature,* XXIII (April 5, 1941), 10.

Clark, Emily. "Appreciation of Ellen Glasgow and Her Work." *Virginia Quarterly Review,* V (April 1929), 182-91.
_____. *Innocence Abroad.* New York: Alfred A. Knopf, 1931, 55-69.
Collins, Joseph. *Taking the Literary Pulse.* New York: Doubleday, Doran and Company, 1924, 68-72.
Cooper, Anice Page. *Authors and Others,* Garden City, New York: Doubleday, Page and Company, 1927, 23-27.
Cooper, Frederic Taber. *Some American Story Tellers.* New York: Henry Holt Company, 1911, 90-111.
_____. "Representative American Story Tellers: Ellen Glasgow." *Bookman,* XXIX (August 1909), 613-18.
Couch, W. T. *Culture in the South.* Chapel Hill: University of North Carolina Press, 1932, passim.
Dabney, Virginius. *Liberalism in the South.* Chapel Hill: University of North Carolina Press, 1932, 361-89.
Freeman, Douglas Southall. "Ellen Glasgow: Idealist." *The Saturday Review of Literature,* XII (August 31, 1935), 11-12.
Gilkyson, Phoebe H. "Points of View." *The Saturday Review of Literature,* VI (November 23, 1929), 467.
Haardt, Sara. "Ellen Glasgow and the South." *Bookman,* LXIX (April 1929), 133-39.
Hatcher, Harlan Henthorne. *Creating the Modern American Novel.* New York: Farrar and Rinehart, Publishers, 1935, 87-98; 21-33.
Jones, Howard Mumford. "The Regional Eminence of Ellen Glasgow," *The Saturday Review of Literature,* XXVI (October 16, 1943), 20.
20.
_____. "The Virginia Edition of the Works of Ellen Glasgow." *New York Herald Tribune Books,* July 24, 1938, 1.
Kazin, Alfred. *On Native Grounds.* New York: Reynal and Hitchcock, 1942, 247-64.
Kilmer, Joyce. *Literature in the Making.* New York: Harper Brothers, 1917, 229-38.
Kohler, Dayton M. "Recognition of Ellen Glasgow." *English Journal,* XXXI (September 1942), 523-29.

Lawrence, Margaret. *School of Femininity*. New York: Frederick Stokes, 1936, 281-310.

Loggins, Vernon. *I Hear America*. New York: Crowell, 1937, 175-94.

Mann, Dorothea Lawrance. "Ellen Glasgow: Citizen of the World." *Bookman*, LXIV (November 1926), 265-71.

Marble, Mrs. Annie (Russell). *A Study of the Modern Novel*. New York: D. Appleton, 1928, 314-18.

Mencken, H. L. "A Southern Skeptic." *American Mercury*, XXIX (August 1933), 504-6.

Mims, Edwin. *The Advancing South*. Garden City, New York: Doubleday Page and Comppany, 1926, 214-28.

————. "The Social Philosophy of Ellen Glasgow." *Social Forces*, IV (March 1926), 495-603.

Monroe, Nellie Elizabeth. *The Novel and Society*. Chapel Hill: University of North Carolina Press, 1941, 139-87.

Overton, Grant M. *Women Who Make Our Novels*. New York: Dodd, Mead and Company, 157-66.

Parker, William R. "Ellen Glasgow: a Gentle Rebel." *English Journal*, XX (March 1931), 187-94.

Pattee, Fred Lewis. *The New American Literature, 1890-1930*. New York: Century, 1930, passim.

Quinn, Arthur Hobson. *American Fiction: an Historical and Crtical Survey*. New York: D. Appleton-Century Company, 1936, 670-79.

Rogers, Cameron. "Realism from the Romantic South." *World's Work*, L (May 1925), 99-102.

Rutherford, Mildred Lewis. *The South in History and Literature*. Atlanta, Georgia: Franklin Turner Company, 1906, 737-38.

Sherman, Stuart Pratt. *Critical Woodcuts*. New York: Scribner, 1926, 73-82.

Van Gelder, Robert. *Writers and Writing*. New York: Scribner, 1946, 319-23.

Wellington, Amy. *Women Have Told, Studies in the Feminist Tradition*. Boston: Little, Brown and Company, 157-73.

Wilson, James Southall. "Ellen Glasgow: Ironic Idealist." *Virginia Quarterly Review*, XV (January 1939), 121-26.

_____. "Ellen Glasgow's Novels." *Virginia Quarterly Review,* IX (October 1933), 595-600.

HISTORY

Beard, Mary Ritter. *America Through Women's Eyes.* New York: Macmillan, 1933, 538-46.
Buck, Paul H. *The Road to Reunion,* 1865-1900. Boston: Little, Brown and Company, 1937.

CHRONOLOGICAL LIST OF THE NOVELS OF ELLEN GLASGOW

The Descendant. 1897.
Phases of an Inferior Planet. 1898.
The Voice of the People. 1900.
The Battle-Ground. 1902.
The Deliverance. 1904.
The Wheel of Life. 1906.
The Ancient Law. 1908.
The Romance of a Plain Man. 1909.
The Miller of Old Church. 1911.
Virginia. 1913.
Life and Gabriella. 1916.
The Builders. 1919.
One Man in His Time. 1922.
Barren Ground. 1925.
The Romantic Comedians. 1926.
They Stooped to Folly. 1929.
The Sheltered Life. 1932.
Vein of Iron. 1935.
In This Our Life. 1941.

Supplemental Bibliography

WORKS OF ELLEN GLASGOW

Beyond Defeat; an Epilogue to an Era. Ed. by Luther Y. Gore.
Charlottesville, Virginia: University Press of Virginia, 1966.
The Collected Stories of Ellen Glasgow. Ed. by Richard K.
Meeker. Baton Rouge: Louisiana State University Press, 1963.
Letters of Ellen Glasgow. Comp. and ed. by Blair Rouse. New
York: Harcourt, Brace and Company, 1958.
The Woman Within. New York: Harcourt, Brace and Company,
1954.

BIBLIOGRAPHY

Kelly, William W. *Ellen Glasgow; a Bibliography.* Charlottesville: University Press of Virginia, 1964.

COMMENTARIES

Godbold, E. Stanley, Jr. *Ellen Glasgow and the Woman Within.*
Baton Rouge: Louisiana State University Press, 1972.
McDowell, F. P. W. *Ellen Glasgow and the Ironic Art of Fiction.*
Madison: University of Wisconsin Press, 1960.
Rouse, Blair. *Ellen Glasgow.* Boston: Twayne Publishers, Inc.,
1963 (Twayne's United States Authors Series).
Rubin, Louis Decimus. *No Place on Earth; Ellen Glasgow, James
Branch Cabell and Richmond-in-Virginia.* Austin: University
of Texas Press, 1959.
Santas, Joan Foster. *Ellen Glasgow's American Dream.* Char-
lottesville: University Press of Virginia, 1965.

3984

PS
3513
L34
Z73

Myer, Elizabeth
Gallup.

The social situation
of women in the
novels of Ellen
Glasgow

DATE			

© THE BAKER & TAYLOR CO.